Returning Vet's Saga

THE HEALING POWER OF POETRY

CHARLIE PETERS

QUILL HAWK PUBLISHING

Returning Vet's Saga: The Healing Power of Poetry

Paperback ISBN: 978-1-965142-32-5
Hardcover ISBN: 978-1-965142-33-2

Library of Congress Control Number: 2024925240

Cover designed by Ava Wood, Fins and Feathers Designs

Quill Hawk Publishing
www.quillhawkpublishing.com

Contents

Introduction

What is contained in this publication is a collection of selected poems that I wrote. I went through a period of being confused and not understanding why I was feeling the way I was and not understanding why I had such great periods of depression, for about fifteen years, after being discharged from the Navy. It seemed my emotions could go from a lion to a lamb and then back again, in an instant. I didn't understand why my set of values was far different than what they had been before I entered the Navy. I didn't talk about what I was feeling, or about what I was experiencing. I kept everything to myself, or at least I thought I kept it to myself.

I was a very light sleeper, to put it mildly. One of my sons invited a friend to spend the night. My son said to his friend, while I was napping on the couch, "Watch this and stand back." He reached out as far as he could and just barely touched my shoulder with his finger. Wha-Zham, I was instantly rising to my feet, with my arms flailing in the air and ready for battle. Then I heard my son and friend laughing nearby. What my son didn't realize was that was how we were awakened on the Sub. No words spoken, so as not to waken anyone else. Touch us on the shoulder and we instantly got out of the rack and went to take care of what we were to do. Some habits die hard.

Sometime in 1990 I purchased a Radio-Alarm-Clock. Then one day, shortly after that, I decided to test the radio alarm. I set it for 2:00 am, and set the radio to a local news channel. The next morning I was up out of bed, like a shot in the dark, when I thought I heard voices in the living room, clear on the other side of the house. I was running as fast as I could, with my fist clenched as hard as it could be. I didn't know what I would encounter, but I was ready for whatever or whoever it was. No intruder was going to survive the night. When I reached the living room no one was in sight and I could distinctly hear the radio blaring away from the alarm I set the night before. All I could do was sit on the couch and laugh out loud, and then the laughter turned to uncontrollable tears. I realized I had a serious problem, but had no idea how to fix it.

Shortly after that I sat down at my computer, and for some unknown reason I just started pounding away at the keyboard. I didn't think about what I was writing. I just let the words flow from my heart, and completely bypass my brain. What came out of that initial writing was the basis of the poem "Returning Vet's Saga." It would take me several years to complete it. Originally it was something I was never going to allow anyone to read; it was just for me. Then I started writing more poetry. Again, it was just for me. The most important lesson I learned was that when I was having an "episode" (for lack of better words) I knew my best poetry would flow with ease, and just letting my heart control my fingers and not my brain.

Eventually, I gave a copy of the completed "Returning Vet's Saga" to a Viet Nam Vet who I was working with and also a good friend. Unbeknownst to me, he then gave it to other Viet Nam Vets, who also worked with us. These other vets came up to me and thanked me. What started out as something personal was now in the hands of others. As these other vets talked with me, I thought, "If my friend has the guts to give the poem to others, then I could do it to." Since then, I have passed out hundreds of copies of that poem to other vets.

What I found was that the feelings I had were not unique, but, they were the same feelings that many others also had.

Our feelings are ours. Whatever they might be, they are not wrong. Our feelings are not something that we need be ashamed of, as I was for many years. Our feelings are a result of what we have experienced throughout our lives. No one should condemn anyone for the feelings they have. For those that might condemn us, their condemnation is a result of their lack of experiencing what we have experienced. If we are condemned for our feelings, then, that condemnation is a result of ignorance, it is not the result of worthwhile knowledge.

Next, with the encouragement of Tom Parker, who was also a Marine who was wounded in action in Viet Nam, I attended a "Viet Nam Veteran's Annual Picnic," held in Anacortes, Washington, every summer. He suggested I bring something that could be auctioned off and the proceeds would be used to send a group of Viet Nam Vets back to Washington D.C. to visit "The Wall." Tom, whom I had previously given a copy of my poem, suggested I put together a book with my poems. Tom said, "I like your poetry and I know the other guys will too." I was not as confident as Tom was, but I told him I would.

It would have been very easy to have just kept my poetry to myself, which was the original intent when I first started writing poetry. It is a very frightening thing to actually let those you know read what you have written. More frightening is to let those you don't know read what one has written. I came up with many excuses for not publishing my poetry; reasons that were valid in my mind. And, the list went on. In fact, my list was getting so large, that I actually waited until the week before the picnic to publish that first collection of poems. But, in the end, I remembered that I had given my word that I would publish the six sets.

I did I put together a book of fifty pages of my poetry. It was the first collection of selected poems that I wrote. That was no small feat. Not the putting together of the poems, but, the putting of them together for others to read. With that release, I opened myself up for others to see me and it was scary. Not for others to see the person on the outside, but, to see the person hidden on the inside. I decided to do that because if I opened myself up and spoke about my feelings, then others might also find a way to speak freely themselves. If only one person finds a way to start speaking freely, then I considered the printing of my poems would be well worth it.

I was very fearful that night before the picnic. I knew I was opening myself up and it was a very uncomfortable feeling. In fact, I didn't sleep. I kept thinking, "I am going to be laughed out of the picnic." And, "What a fool he is." That was the way I felt.

Sooner than I thought picnic day was here. As soon as I placed my six sets on the auction table, various ones came up, took them off the table and started reading from them. Not just a few, but many. Then I was asked to select a poem to read myself or have someone else read. I told them that I couldn't read it, but I selected the poem titled "At His Best" to be read. As the auctioneer read the poem, I noticed that it became very quiet, almost too quiet, and the reader's voice became choked up at times. Then the six sets were auctioned off. I could not believe that others actually wanted my work and they were willing to pay for it. The going price that day was $25.00 a book.

I thought, at first, those that came up to me and said they enjoyed my poetry, were just being kind. Others said I should publish my poetry, but I thought they just wanted to make me feel good.

The vets at the picnic made me feel the best I had felt in a long time. The encouragement they gave me at the picnic moved me to again publish another set of poems for that Annual Viet Nam Veterans Picnic. I published six volumes of poetry for the "Annual Viet Nam Veterans Picnic," at Anacortes, Washington for the years 1998, 1999, 2000, and 2001. Each year the volumes sold for more than they had the previous year. The volumes sold for $25 each in 1998, and they went for more each subsequent year. Finally in 2001 the last volume on the table was auctioned off for $50. The profits all went for a great cause and not one penny went into my pocket.

Here was the introduction to that first release.

"This release has been published for survivors. That has only recently been a term that I have realized applies to myself and all others that are still alive. We survived a war, we survived ridicule and condemnation after the war, we are surviving our inner most fears, we have survived night mares and cold sweats, and we have survived the temptation to end it all. If you are reading this publication, then you are a survivor, because if you had not survived up to this point, you would not be around to be reading this. For those that are reading this, don't just read it, but add to it. This release is not an end, it is a beginning. This release is not a solution, but, rather, it is the beginning of a new road that can be traveled. A road that can be traveled where we express ourselves, not a road we travel in silence. It is not the destination, but, rather, the journey that makes life's roads worth traveling."

We are the sum total of all our experiences. The Viet Nam War was one experience. In this collection of poems I also included some poetry that is about some of life's other experiences. I have found poetry can be a beautiful way of expressing oneself.

I do feel compelled to mention another person that took my poetry where I never thought it would go. That person is Amy M. Le. She is an author and she wrote a trilogy of books about the treatment of Vietnamese and Viet Nam Veterans. In her second book, *Snow in Seattle,* she included a whole chapter where my poem "Return Vet's Saga" was included and giving me full credit for writing the poem. If she can include my poem in her book then why in the world should I not publish a book about my poetry?

A Man Less Than His Best

This poem I dedicate to my family, my wife and my children, who have only known me when I was less than my best.

Photo taken when Charlie was at his best in Gymnastics! The maneuver is called a "Stutz to Handstand," on the Parallel Bars.

There once was a man, who was at his best.
Proud he was, while at his best.
Friends he had, who were at his side.
Proud they were, while he was at his best.

Crowds they once cheered, for this man at his best.
Awards he received, for being his best.
Proud was this man, who was at his best.
And proud were his friends, proud of this man who was at his best.

Then a war, it did come for this man at his best.
This man did fight, this man, who had been at his best.
Then this man, who had been at his best, became this man,
no longer at his best.
He then became, as some would say, a man who was less than his best.

Then a wife, he would come to have.
A wife he would have, while he was less than his best.
A man she would have and only knew, while he was less than his best.
This wife of his would get a man, less than his best.
What this wife of his would get, would be a man, that once was his best,
But she would not see him at his best, she would see, only what was left.

To that wife of his, he is so sorry,
That she only saw what was left,
And never knew this man when at his best.

He is so sorry she only knew what was left.
Oh, if only she could have known, this man at his best.
How proud she would have been, of this man at his best!

Then children they would come to have, children they would love,
Children who would only know, this man who was less than his best.
His children would think, this man was best,
But his children would never know,
This man at his best, they would just know what was left.

To those children of his,
He is so sorry that they only knew what was left,
And they never knew this man when at his best,
He is so sorry they only knew what was left.

Oh, if only they could have known, this man at his best.
How proud they would have been, of this man at his best!
To that family of his, both wife and children alike,
He wishes they could have known him when he was at his best.

He is sorry they never saw him at his best,
He is sorry that they only saw what was left!
He loves dearly, that family of his,
Because they love him for what was left,
And not for what was once his best!

This man, who once was his best,
Would come to know, that the best he could be now,
Was not the best, he had once been, but only the best, of what was left.

What was left, was not a man at his best.
What was left, was a man in his shell,
Not a man, who was once at his best.

Try as he might, and try as he could,
This man, once at his best,
Would now have to settle for only second best.

Now were gone, for this man, once at his best.
The crowds and the friends, who were once so proud of this man at his best,
But, sad to say, they never knew him when he was less than his best,
They never knew what was left.

Now this man would become, the best of what was left,
Not the best he could have been, but, the best of what was left!
This man never dreamed he would not be his best,
This man never dreamed he would only be what was left!

But, the best of what is left,
May actually be better than what once was his best!
Only time will tell which actually turns out best,
What was once his best or what is left!

The Three Walked Together

This poem is dedicated to the memory of William (Buddy) Leander Erickson, Jr. (graduated from Foster High School 1966, K.I.A. 10/05/1969) and Ed Hock (graduated from Foster High School 1967, K.I.A. 02/12/1969). Both were Killed in Action in the Vietnam War. The three of us walked home together during our high school days. Here is the poem of remembrance.

The three walked home together, from school they did walk together.
Their futures they did plan as they walked together.
Their hopes and dreams they did share, as they walked together.
Joke and laugh they did, as they walked together.

Friends they were, for a lifetime they thought, as they walked together.
Never was their talk of war, as the three walked together.
Never was their talk of death, as the three walked together.
Never was their talk of a time they might not walk together.

From high school they did leave, those three boys who walked together.
Then they found themselves in war, these three boys who walked together.
Overnight from boys to men they became,
These three boys who had walked together.
Never did they realize that the three of them
Would never walk together again.

The three never talked about the war, as they once walked together.
Two would die, killed in action they were,
Two of the three who had walked together.
Only one returned, to walk alone,
The three of them never to walked together again.
Two lifetimes one has lived, since the other two lost their lives.

Of the three that walked together, only one was to vote.
Only one was to marry and only one was to have children.
Of the three that walked together,
Two never voted, married or had children.

Of the three that walked together, only the one remembers
The walks the three of them had together.
The one remembers the two, who lost their lives.
But, all should remember all those who gave their lives.

Now, all in the nation and country, should never forget the two,
Nor forget all the others, who gave of their lives
So that all might walk together in peace and harmony.

A memorial we do have, only one day a year it is,
To remember those who gave of their lives,
So that the rest might walk together!
The one has never forgot, how the three used to walk together.
Now only the one is left,
To walk alone with the memories of when the three once walked together!

William L. "Buddy" Erickson, Jr.
Date of Birth: 05/13/1948
Graduated High School 1966
Seattle, Washington
Branch of Service: U.S. Army
Date KIA October 5, 1969
Panel/Line on the Wall: 17W/43

Leldon Edwin "Ed" Hock, Jr.
Date of Birth: 10/22/1948
Graduated High School 1967
Seattle, Washington
Branch of Service: U.S. Army
Date KIA February 12, 1969
Panel/Line on the Wall: 32W/20

Photos are taken from their high school yearbooks, respective senior year. Now you will be forever remembered my friends.

Three Words

This poem is dedicated to all combat Vets who so longed to be hugged and loved after returning from patrol, whether the patrol was on land, sea or air!

Returning from patrol, where death and I stared face to face,
My prayer was it to die and end the fright inside,
Or was it to live to be frightened again?

Returning from patrol, my thoughts inside how much more can I endure,
How many more times can I do this,
Before it is my last time?

Returning from patrol, three words that were longed to hear,
I miss you, I love you, I want to see you.

Who would say these three words?
Who would care to say these three words?
Would I live to hear these three words?

Would I hear from someone I knew these three words,
Would someone I knew care to say these words?

No, that was not the way it would prove to be.
These words I did come to hear,
But, not from someone close to me,
Not from someone who knew me.

These three words I did come to hear,
From a stranger they did come to my ear,
From someone I would never see again, these three words I did hear.

The stranger did not care,
The stranger did not say them in sincerity,

But, the stranger did say these three words to me.
To hear these three words, did keep me in touch with reality.

These three words I never forgot,
But the person that said them has long been forgotten.
The people I do remember,
I never remember them saying these three words.

So, why do I remember the ones that did not say these three words?
And, yet forget those who said these three words,
These three words that I so longed to hear?
And those words were "I Love You!"

Away

While I was away, you stayed behind.
While I was training for war, you were training for a work.
While I was fighting in a war, unsure and insecure was I.
You were working a job, home safe and secure.

While I was at war, facing death and the worst it could bring.
You were facing life, and the best it could bring.

While I was at war, living in a bunk, you were back home building a home.
While I was away, not seeing family nor friends,
You were back home, busy making a family and friends.

While I was away, looking for a place to hide,
You were home, safe and secure inside.
While I was away, you were able to get ahead.

Then, I returned,
To find you were climbing the ladder to success up ahead,
I was just looking for work to try to stay ahead.

Now, that I have returned,
Will I ever catch up and get ahead?
Will I ever catch up, to be where I would if I had not went away?

Young and Innocent

Young and innocent I once used to be.
Plans for the future, I was making for me.
College was for me, to work on what I could be.
For college all said, is where you need to be,
So you can become whatever you will be.

Summers and weekends I worked,
To pay for my education,
So a job I could get,
Would provide for my needs.

My part time job was safe and secure.
And pay for my last year at school it would.
In return, for them I would work
For the next five years.

To the Olympics, hopefully I would go.
Four hours a day I trained for that goal.

Good I was getting, but I had not reached my goal.
Competing I was and better I was getting.
Injury and work had not stopped me from training.

Then my training, my education it would pay,
No need for part time work to help with living.
A full ride it was called, now on top, I thought I was.
With nothing to stop me from reaching my goals.

How good I felt,
The Olympics in sight,
And a secure job waiting.

Then all of a sudden,
A lottery I did win!
Number forty-seven meant my world would shatter.

Shatter it did,
When in May a letter I did receive.
To the Army you will go, to serve where you are needed.
No choice do you have, but to go when you are asked.

So in June of 1969 I did go as asked.
No Olympics for me, not even a chance to try anymore.
No secure job, anymore was for me,
Your education will stop, for we need you now.

Sorry I was,
For dreams and goals were now shattered and gone.

But, go as asked I did,
For country and God.
For the rest of my life,
To wonder how far I would have gone,
And what I would have reached.

Before going to serve as asked,
All wanted me.
Now that I am back,
All have forgotten what I could have been.
Now I must fight to live on again.

Being a Vet

Being a vet is a great thing to be.
From the Revolutionary War a group we started to be.
After that war, every generation has added their number
To that group that was to be.

From all walks of life they became a group that walked as one.
Each group that gathered as one,
Fought in wars and found they were mightier than one.
And they all came to know that it was "One for All and All for One."

In wars they all have fought, some were small and others were great.
Not all that fought made it back,
Some never returned so that Vets they became.
For those that returned, part of a fine group they became-
Veterans they became.

That group of fighting young men,
Became part of a group known as veterans.

Stories they could tell, but mostly they didn't,
Except when they gathered together as the veterans they are.

When gathered together, stories they would share,
Memories in their past once again become alive,
Just like it was once in the past.
They always remember those who through a war did not last.

All should remember that fine group of men
Who once went to war for freedom for us all
They gave it their best, to defend us all.

They fought with their lives and gave up their blood,
So that freedom might be ours and ours for all time to come.
They have done all that and for that veterans they have become.

The Big Man Came Back

There was a big man, and very strong was he,
This big man was a hero, in the war he fought over there,
A war he came back from, with medals on his chest.
The wounds he received, he survived from all that.

When he returned, a sweet heart he did meet.
This pretty young thing was also petite at that.
Her beauty excelled, and was far above all those around.
Finally they married, in a land she called home.

This big man and her, plans they did make,
For a future that looked bright.
A family they planned, and children they had.
Closer they became, when their babies they arrived.

Then at the height of their new found bliss,
The son was injured, in an accident that almost cost him his life.

Care the son needed, so the big man sent him where care could be had.
This big man was sad, because his son had been hurt.

All was not lost, for this big man and wife,
They still had their daughter and their son would recover.
When the son had recovered, new plans were made,
For all four of them at last, together they would be, forever to last.

But, soon, new sadness would come for this big man,
Who had already seen too much, in what sadness could bring.
Now, that petite, pretty wife of this big man disappeared,
And she was nowhere to be found.

Gone were the plans, this big man had made.
What once was so bright was now gone for this big man.
What could he do, so that the two would have,
The best that could be had.

But, that big man was cut to the heart, what would he do.
With nowhere to turn, the two he let go, and separate they would be.
Now, the family of four was a family no more.
All that was left was this big man alone.

Life did not last for that family of four,
Gone were the wife, and the children that were two.
That big, strong man, was now broken at last.
A heart once so full was now empty at last.

In a short while, that empty heart finally gave out.
Now, gone were the man and the wife,
Now, gone were the plans and the future so bright.
All that was left was the two that were brought forth.

Boot Camp

Whatever it was called, Boot Camp, Basic Training, or Flight Training, it was the life of a new recruit; a new recruit into the military life. It took that early training, which was ten to sixteen weeks to change the recruits from civilians to a fighting military machine. During that several week period, the former identity was lost; that former identity that had taken a life time to make. The former identity was replaced with a new one, which was the identity that the military wanted one to have. There were no choices, it was change and be like the rest.

Boot Camp and Charlie is bottom row, 3rd from right

At first you arrived, so quiet and shy.
Frightened at first, no one do you know.
For ten weeks you will stay, a lifetime it seems.
From civilian you change, to a fighting machine you become.

The change is not slow, but rapidly it takes place.
The first to go is all the hair you once had.
Close to the head, no stubble is seen.

Then the civvies are replaced with new uniforms.
Quickly you find that new is not clean,
All that you're issued has to be stenciled and washed
Then neatly folded, with creases in the proper places.

Then comes the day, when personal identity is lost,
That is the day when heads are shaved,
And "all" hair is lost.
All look the same, whether they are short, tall, skinny or fat.

That was only the start,
Next all humility is lost,
Where recruits are lower than dirt.
What was once a man, is now a robot, to be retrained for a new art.

The new art, which all are preparing for,
Is the art of warfare, an art which they were well trained for.
An art, which would never be lost,
Nor one that would be replaced, for what was before.

Everything in order and in the lockers rightly placed,
For soon comes inspection, and all ends up on the floor.
Soon you do learn, no exceptions are allowed.
All in a proper place, and proper place for all.

Everything is regimented, all is the same.
Up at reveille and lights out at taps.
Taps does not mean sleep,
It means work without light, and quiet at that.
No choices do you have, you are told what to do.

No place do you go
A bunk is not made, unless a quarter from it can bounce.

Remember to write home,
It is an order you know.

Pictures we see and movies we watch,
Where an enemy is bad,
The enemy needs to be stopped,
And his evils not spread!

All are convinced that we must do our part.
No one would want such evils to be here.
Those evils must be stopped, from right where they are.
Those evils must be stopped, before they ever reach here.

Then comes a day, when talk is about war.
All are told that some will go now,
Directly to combat is where they will be,
And some will die and not return back home, where you wanted to be!

Then the final day arrived,
Orders we are given, to one and all alike.
To all parts of the earth, all would depart.
Never to know what happened, to those we had been with!

Boys

Boys they were, who were asked to fight.
A few were 17, more were 18 and many were 19.
Not old enough to vote or drink.

Many not old enough to even think about marriage.
And even more never thought about buying a house.
Some had not even had a job.

They were just boys, not yet even thought of as men.
But, it would not be long and men they would become.
For boys enter a war, but no boys come out of a war.

During war these boys would be aged far beyond their friends,
They would even age beyond that of their fathers.
They would age far beyond their time.

A day at war ages one by more than a month at peace.
Now, those who were boys, not so many months ago,

Now became men, more experienced at life
And surviving, than those back home.

A few months in war adds years to one's life,
What once was a smooth face becomes weather beaten and sun baked.
Once innocent eyes, can now stare into space.

A few months before they had never fired a gun.
Now, they are shooting and killing all that is in sight.
Once afraid of fighting, they soon become calloused about killing.

Not so long ago the only danger they faced
Was crossing the street as they stopped, looked and listened.
Now they are ducking and dropping, for no reason at all.

Not so long ago the worst they had seen
Was a cut from a saw.
Now, they have seen others without heads, hands, arms, feet and legs.

Now, they are not boys anymore, not boys anymore at all.
Now, they are men—aged far beyond their time.
While their friends back home are still boys and no more than that.

That Big Brother of Mine

There were over 59,479 (latest count) U.S. Service Members who lost their lives in the Viet Nam War. But, that is only the tip of the iceberg. Each one of those had families that were also affected; a wife or girlfriend, some had children, a mother, a father, brothers, sisters, aunts, uncles, cousins, and friends. It was not just surviving veterans that suffered the loss of the 59,479. Veterans only knew the dead vet for a few months, and the loss for them was never forgotten. But, never forget, each vet who died had a family and friends that had known them for a lifetime. Those family and friends lost someone that had been near and dear to them for twenty years. Those family members and friends also suffered a great loss. This poem is dedicated to the family and friends of those that were slain in Viet Nam and those that later lost their lives as a result of that war.

Oh, brother of mine, how great you were.
So very kind you were, so very thoughtful you were,
Though bigger than me, you treated me well, big brother of mine.

I will never forget that day you went away.
The day you left to fight, in a war so far away.
You wrote home, from that war so far away.

In your letters to home, you always asked about me.
You never talked about what the war was like over there.
You never talked about what you saw over there.

Then one day, that captain came by.
He told us that you had been killed in that war over there.
He told us a hero you had been over there.

I never did think that could happen to you,
No, I never did think that would happen to you.
You were so big, strong and powerful, Oh, big brother of mine.

I was so sure you would return from that war
And I never did tell you how much you really meant to me
I don't think I told you how much I really did love you,
Which I regret to this day!

It was not a dead hero that I wanted back home.
It was my big brother, alive and well, that I wanted back home.
I wanted more than just a memory of you, I wanted you back,
Oh, big brother of mine!

I remember the day, you returned back over here.
In a casket you were laid, when they brought you back home.
How natural you looked, others did say.

But, I will always remember how unnatural you looked to me.
Your hair parted on the left side, when right it used to be!
Those white gloves on your hands, how you detested them so.

Though that happened more than twenty-five years ago,
And many more have gone by the way, since that last day I saw you.
You were the last one I viewed, no others have I viewed,
Before they were laid down to rest.

I have never forgotten you, Oh big brother of mine.
The memory of you will always be clear,
You never stopped being that big brother of mine.
You were great, and I miss you, Oh big brother of mine.

That Broken Down Man

Here is another poem about veterans returning home, no matter what war they have fought. Many returning vets feel like things will be like they were before. But on returning back home this picture is how Country and Men made them feel!

Here is another poem about veterans returning home, no matter what war they have fought.

As you looked deep into the eyes of that man,
You could see he once had been a very proud man.
But, now as you looked at that broken down man,
You could see the spirit had finally been broken in that man.

As you now looked at that broken down man,
You could see he once stood tall and straight, as a man.
But as you now looked at that broken down man,
All you could see was a stooped shouldered man.

As you now looked at that broken down man,
You could tell he once held his head high, as a fine man,
But now as you looked at that broken down man,
All you could see was his head held low, as a beaten down man.

As you now looked at that broken down man,
You could tell he once smiled and was happy inside,
But now as you looked at that broken down man,
All you could see was a sad man inside.

As you now looked at that broken down man,
You could tell he once could fight back, as a very strong man.
But now as you looked at that broken down man,
All you could see was a spirit, which was gone out of that broken down man.

As you now looked at that broken down man,
You wonder what had went wrong with that man,
What ever happened to that broken down man?

Why was he torn and so forlorn, as a man, why was he down,
And now a broken down man.

In war he was honored, as a hero of a man and a powerful man,
But after the war, all have forgotten and now he's a broken down man,
No one remembers he was once not a broken down man.

That broken down man had been beaten down, by his fellow man.
He had been thrown around, by his fellow man.
Had been tossed aside and broken down, by his fellow man.

In the end what do you see?
That broken down man was the man in the mirror, in the mirror on the wall.
In the mirror on the wall, can be seen that broken down man,
After all it was I, who is that broken down man, in the mirror on the wall.

The Cave in My Mind

Entrance to "The Cave in my Mind"

There is a place I can go,
To escape from my troubles and problems that I often now face.
There I can go any time I please and stay as long as I want or need.
I can go there as often as I want or need.

This place is the cave in my mind.
What a pleasant place to go, this retreat I have made.
The floor of this cave with sand it is lined, that from the sun is heated.
The sand as warm as a fire it is, also so soft on my back.

There is a rock, so soft and worn it has become.
A place to lay my head, so rest I can get.
There is a stream in this cave, over rocks it is running,
Soft and gentle music it is making.
Relaxing music to my mind and ears it is.

This stream feeds a pool, a pool that is warm and refreshing,
In it my feet are resting and relaxing.

The walls of this cave with flowers and trees of all sorts it is lined.
A sweet fragrance is added and with it the cave is so filled!
Flowers with so many colors and shapes,

So pleasing to see in this cave in my mind.
Trees throughout that make the air fresh,
Are by the walls in this cave in my mind.

Now and then animals enter this cave in my mind,
So pleasing and comforting to watch them play all around.

Occasionally, I allow a kind, gentle person to enter
Whose voice is so soft, gentle and kind.
They come within the walls of my cave saying
"You're all right and all will be fine."
A person who listens intently to the words I do say.

Relax that person's voice does say,
Remember you are loved and needed they call to my mind.
Your fine and things will get better, they consolingly remind me.

No harsh words are spoken in that cave in my mind.
So pleasant to stay, in that cave of my mind.
Why ever return to this world that is harsh, violent and unkind?

When I am in this cave in my mind, don't call me out,
Let me stay for as long as I want.
Don't worry, for I will return, when I am refreshed and well, all in good time.

If you dare to relax, come join me in this cave in my mind.
You too, may find the peace that is there to enjoy.
If you dare take a chance, help make this place we are in,
Like the cave in my mind!

Charlie

War does some strange things to people. Before I was drafted I was called "Charlie." After I was discharged from the Navy I didn't allow anyone to call me Charlie anymore. It was not something I did intentionally; I just didn't feel comfortable being called Charlie. After I was discharged I was called Chuck. For over fifteen years I was called "Chuck." Then one day I was talking with an old high friend, who also served in the Navy during the same period I had served. I called him by the name I remembered him by and he corrected me, saying: "I am not called that anymore!" Then we talked about why we were now called by different names. Since, I have learned that many changed the name they were called after they were discharged from the military. It is possible that our old names reminded of something we once were, something that we no longer were, and changing our names helped ease the pain of what we would never be again.

CHARLIE PETERS

Off to war Charlie went,
Many friends saying, "We'll miss you while you are over there,"
And we will be true to you here,
While you are fighting the war over there.

Companions a many, he had when he left for over there,
All saying, "Hurry back home and we'll party back over here."
Friends, how good they once were,
And a party they did have here, before he left for war over there.

In words and intents, they were good over here.
But while Charlie was gone over there,
The friends they soon left back over here!

Soon Charlie was dead and Chuck was alive.
Poor Chuck, friends he had none, they had all gone by the way,
For no one now cared for Chuck,
Who they thought had now gone very astray.

Then Chuck did return back over here,
With Charlie still gone, when he came back here.
Old Charlie would try to jump out,
But, Chuck would say "No" and protect him once again.

Old friends, to Chuck they would say,
You we know not, you're not like Charlie who once went away.
Charlie we once knew well, in a very fine way.

To Chuck they would speak, you're not like the Charlie,
whose memory we keep.
You're not friendly and fun, like Charlie we loved, before he went away.
Chuck is so strong, for all to see, Charlie is hidden, so none can see.

Will Charlie ever come out, for others to see?
Or will Chuck keep him hidden, so none dare to see?
Charlie wants out, so he can live once again,
Who will help Charlie to live once again?

The Color of Angels

There are some, maybe even many,
That doubt the existence of angels.
No amount of evidence will convince them otherwise.

I, on the other hand, need no convincing.
A lifetime of evidence has been given to me.
Over a lifetime I have learned what color angels are,
They are the same color as those messengers they use!

For those that have been used by angels,
You are truly blessed,
Whether you were used knowingly or unknowingly.

In a moment of despair, a tear I did shed,
At that very moment a comforting word you did offer.
Those words were angelic to my ears.

As I glanced at you, I then noticed your color
Your color, it was black
And the angel behind you must have also been black.

Then in a moment of tragedy,
When I was about to lose my life,
You reached out and grabbed me,
Throwing me in the direction of safety.

As I glanced over I noticed you were white,
And the angel behind you
Must have also been white.

At a time in life, when I needed it most
There you were and love you gave to me.
As I glanced over I noticed you were brown,
And the angel behind you must have also been brown.

When at a time a kind expression I needed,
There you were with a kind expression to give.
Your hand reached out and comfort you gave.

As I glanced over to you I noticed you were yellow,
And the angel behind you must have also been yellow.

Yes, I can tell you the color of angels,
By the colors of those messengers they use.

Angels are the colors of the rainbow,
They are the colors of a beautiful flower garden.
They are the colors in the sky,
From dawn to dusk and then on into the night.

Whatever color my next angel is, is not important,
Because I know they can use a messenger,
Who any color they might be.

It is not their color that is important,
But it is the message their messengers bring.
The message is what is most important after all.

In the end, color is after all,
A kind word, a gentle expression,
Or a lifesaving gesture.

It is now easy for me to understand
That angels are any color and every color.

So, too, with the messengers angels use,
They are any color and every color.

If you doubt this, just take the time to look around
And notice their messengers of many colors
And how those messengers give comfort to people of all color.

Changed in a Day

In June of 1969 I was drafted. Rather than be drafted, I chose to enlist in the Navy. Thus my military life started three days before I was to be drafted and it lasted four years longer than if I had been drafted. It was to replace the existing draft system and was supposed to be fairer for all. All would be left up to the draw of a number.

Life was so good, with choices all mine to make.
That all changed in a day.
A day I remember and can never forget.

That was the day where my life ended as mine.
That was the day, the choices stopped being mine.
That was the day I belonged to my country
And no longer did I belong to me!

That was the day, no more choices did I have.
That was the day, choices were taken away.
That was the day, only orders would I have.

That was the day, when life stopped to exist.
That was the day; I was told what to do.
That was the day; I was told where to go.
That was the day; my life was no longer mine.

It was a day, orders I did take.
It was a day, orders I obeyed.
It was a day, orders I carried out well.

The change was complete.
So complete was that change, that never would I change back.
Never would I be the same, when the choices were again mine to make.

I was changed in a day and would never change back.

I Did Not Come Back

I remember a man, so long ago it was.
That man I once knew is now a total stranger to me.
Sometimes I think about that man, I once knew.

I often think about that man and what he used to be.
He was friendly to one and all,
And many called him their friend, after all.

As I think about that man, I once knewso far back in the past
I remember his many accomplishments and how he thought they would last.
And the awards he received for the things he had done in his past.

On other occasions, I remember the dreams he had and what he hoped for
And the goals he had set and the dreams he was reaching for.

Many a time he surprised those around him, and even himself,
For what he was able to do.
I remember that a hard worker he used to be.

And how he worked hard to make his dreams come true,
To become what he wanted to be.

I remember what he hoped he would become
And what he thought he would be
And how he was becoming what he wanted to be
And how others were proud of what he was becoming
And what they thought he would someday be.

Yes, I remember much about that man, I once knew.
But he is not the same man he used to be; he is not the man I once knew.
And that man he used be, is now a stranger to him,
He is just someone he once knew.

That man, who is now a stranger to him,
Was that man he once knew.
And was that man he was before, before he went to war.

When he came back from war
He was a stranger to all he once knew,
But most of all, he was a stranger to himself
Because he was no longer the man he once knew.

That man he once knew was the man he used to be, a long time before.
That man he once did know is now a stranger to him;
He is not at all like before.
Because, he did not come back the same,
The same as he was before!

The Difference

I went into the military in 1969 and was discharge in 1975. Great changes took place during that six year period. Changes that I still do not completely understand.

When I got out, jobs were so few,
Not plentiful, like they were once before.
Work was hard to get, not easy like before!
Many were laid off, not just a few like before.

When I got out,
People worked so hard, but didn't play like before.
No one enjoyed what was around, like they once did before.

When I got out, the times were so poor,
Now people had to have two jobs or more,
Just to make ends meet.
Not just one job, like it was once before.

When I got out, many women were working,
Few were at home, like they once were before.
Those that were working would now swear up a storm,
Not well mannered, like they once were before.

When I went in, houses were plenty.
To own or to rent, not much did it cost.

When I got out, the difference was great,
So great was the difference, the shock was too much.

When I got out,
The jobs they were few,
Instead of the many they once were.
Jobs were hard to get, not easy like before.

When I got out,
You could not just say, "Work I do need,"
Like it once used to be.

When I got out,
Many had to work, two or more,
Just to make ends meet,
And not play anymore, like once before.

When I got out,
It was not safe, like it was before.
People locked doors; they were not open like before.

When I got out,
Tension filled the air; it was not calm like before.
People were not friendly, like they once were before.
Yelling and screaming, no kindness like before.

When I got out,
Children were running loose, not controlled like before.
Adults were running scared, not leading like before.
Families were torn apart, not close like before.

When I got out,
Many women did work,
Few at home, like once before.

When I got out,
Your language you did watch, when women were around,
However, now women would swear, not like before.

When I got out,
Houses were no more, like it was before.
Few could now buy, like they once did before.
Rent was so high, not low like it was before.

When I got out, the world had changed, it was not like before.
People were not friendly, like they were once before.
Now they did fight, like never before.

CHARLIE PETERS

When I got out,
What I remembered was to be found no more.
The home I left was not the same anymore.
What I did see, was much worse than before.

When I got out, oh, what a great change had taken place,
Such a great change, it was surely not like before.
The shock of my life,
Was to move on ahead and not live like before!

Why couldn't it have been the same, like it was once before?
Why couldn't it have been the same, like I remembered before?
Why couldn't it have been the same, when I came back from war?

The Flag

It's a piece of cloth that with a gentle breeze so softly blowing,
waves in the air.
It's red, white and blue, for all to see, waving gently in the air.
But it's more than a piece of cloth, that's waving in the air.

That piece of cloth stands for many of things,
It stands for freedom for all those it is representing.
It stands for those,
Who into battle went many times with that piece of cloth they were carrying.

It stands for those, who in battle with that piece of cloth were defending.
It stands for those,
Whose lives were lost while that piece of cloth they were holding.
It stands for those, who for that piece of cloth were sacrificing.

It stands for all those who gave it their best and gave it their all.
It stands for those who defended those that did not have to answer the call.
It stands for those who follow, so that they might have it all.

It stands for the dreams that something better will come after all.
It stands for the freedom of all,
So none will be afraid and all can stand so very tall.
It stands for the hope that there will be justice for all.

When we see that flag waving in the air,
We all need to stand and remember this all.
We need to show respect for that piece cloth, that really does represent us all.
We need to be in awe, for that flag is more than a piece of cloth,
but it is a part of us all.

Flee or Fight

We inherit a 'flee or fight' instinct, when we are born. The instinct works naturally, but it can either be enhanced (to better protect us) or reprogrammed or retrained. That instinct is supposed to protect us from harm. If it is reprogrammed, then we no longer have a built in, "God Given," self-protection system. That instinct can either be retrained so that we always flee, or we always fight. In other words, the natural "flee or fight" instinct becomes either a "flee only" or a "fight only" instinct. For those that have served in the military, and especially combat veterans, that natural "flee or fight" instinct was retrained to be a "fight only" instinct. When the vets were discharged from the military, they were never retrained. The fight only instinct they had was not reprogrammed to be a "flee or fight" instinct. This "fight" instinct they now had would follow them for the rest of their lives, unless at some point they were reprogrammed to a "flee or fight" instinct. This "fight instinct" would be carried over into every aspect of their lives. Their only reaction to any confrontation would be to "fight," whether it was verbal or physical.

*Their natural instinct is now to fight; it is an instinct that enabled
them to survive a war. Without reprogramming they know no other
response; it is fight only. Fleeing is not an option.*

When I was born, an instinct I had
To flee or fight it was.
As I grew this instinct also grew
To help me through life and trouble.

Then drafted I was.
Re-trained I was to fight, fleeing no longer an option.
Trained to fight, even when fleeing is what I should do.

So my flee or fight instinct, became a fight or fight instinct.
Flee I could not, fight I had to.
No longer a choice could I make.
It was now fight at all cost, and never to flee.

When I came back, fighting was my instinct,
Fleeing no longer possible.
So, now when trouble arises
Fleeing is no choice, only fighting I can do.

How nice fleeing once was.
But now no fleeing for me, fighting is all I can do.
Oh how I would like, to learn to FLEE and not to fight.
But, who will now teach me to flee instead of fight?

For I was once taught to fight,
But, never re-taught to flee.
I no longer have a choice, but fighting I must.

Freedom's Not Another Word

When I was young I only thought freedom was another word.
No meaning did it really have.
I only thought it's something free, I didn't know it's a price to pay
I thought it came without a price.

And if it came without a price, then its value there was none.
If it's value it had none, then its meaning was obscure.
If freedom we have always had, then it's just another word
With no meaning that's understood.

But, when freedom I didn't have, then meaning it began to have.
Because one can never realize, that freedom's not another word
Until freedom they no longer have, then freedom's meaning they soon realize.

Then freedom's not another word, freedom has a price to pay.
The price one pays for freedom now means that freedom isn't free.
But, that freedom has a cost, and the cost is very high.

Lives are lost to pay that price and war is fought to win the prize
The prize we have is freedom now, and freedom comes with such a price.
That its meaning we'll now realize, it's a price that's worth the cost.

There are many that lost their life, so that freedom's ours for life.
They gave their lives so all might have freedom for all their life
There are also those that gave, so that freedom we enjoy
They gave the arms and legs they had, it was a cost they willing paid
So that freedom we would have and only a word it wouldn't be
So that freedom would always be, a way of life for you and me

When we understand its price, then freedom's values are worth the cost.
And for those that that paid the price, then freedom's not another word.
Then freedom now is realized, to be a word that's highly prized.

For those that paid the price so high, the price they paid so others can have
The freedom that is cherished by all.
Even though no price they paid, but someone's paid the price for them.
No greater honor is for man, but to pay the price for them
For Freedom's gain for all of us.

But, for those that paid the price, then freedom's not another word,
Freedom's now theirs for life and freedom's now a word to prize
And freedom's not another word, but freedom is a way of life
So its meaning is understood, and it means it's with a price
And its price is worth the cost, so all might have what it means
And enjoy their freedom now, freedom that should be dear to all.

And no one can ever say to them, the price for freedom I paid for you.
No one's paid the price for me, that price I paid by myself.
Now, I've earned the right to say, the price for freedom I've paid myself.
I paid that price for all of us, so all of us could freedom know.

And now I have pride myself, because I know I paid the price
The price for freedom for all to have, the price for freedom to be called their
own
The price I paid because I know, freedom's not just another word
Freedom is a way of life and the price is worth the cost.

And, freedom's now a way of life, and freedom describes that way of life.
Now, freedom's not another word, freedom is a way of life.
A way of life I can enjoy, because the price I've paid myself
The price I paid because I served, in time of war it was I served.

And my life I could have lost, but since I didn't lose my life
Now I've earned the right to have and enjoy my freedom now
And enjoy it for my life.

Freedom's not another word, freedoms now a way of life
That I can now enjoy for life,
Because the price I paid myself and I've earned the right myself,
To have my freedom for my life

Not so young in years I am, now I really understand
Freedom's not another word and freedom's not just a word,
Now I really know for sure, freedom is a way of life
And its price is surely high, but I'm glad I paid the price

Because, now I know what it means and its meaning I'll always prize
Because, now I know it's a word, it's a word that's highly prized
And its price was paid with lives

Now I know I'm not alone, and in pride I now do stand.
With all of those the price they've paid, for the freedom called our own,
I do stand with all of those, who have fought in all the wars,
So that freedom is a word, but it's not just a word.

So freedoms always a way of life, and I know others will stand
When they too will answer the call, and they will learn as I
That freedom's not just a word, but it's really a way of life.

And its cost is worth the price, so all might have that way of life
That freedom's came to me for us, for those living and those to come.
Freedom's price is worth the cost
And I'm proud I can say I have paid the price so dear
So freedom can stay for life.

When I Got Out

When I got out,
This is what I had been told,
No one will be there waiting for you,
No one will be there cheering for you.

When I got out,
This is what I had been told,
Tell no one where you have been or what you have done!
If you do talk, to court you will go,
Not civilian, but to a military court you will surely go!

When I got out
This is what I should have been told
No one will be there, welcoming you back.
No one will hug you or want you to be back.

When I got out
This is what I should have been told

No friends will you have,
And no friends will you make.
You'll not be remembered, but forgotten you will.

When I got out
This is what I should have been told
No job will you have,
And to find one will be hard!
One job you will not keep,
But many you will have.

When I got out
This is what I should have been told
Jobs you don't like, is what you will have.
The job you do want, you will not be able to have
You will work fast, and be told to slow down.
You will help others, but never be helped.

When I got out
This is what I should have been told
You will be expected to know what you do,
But others they will teach, what they need to do.

When I got out
This is what I should have been told
Retirement you would like,
But most likely not have!

When I got out
This is what I should have been told
A boss you will have, but you he will not like,
When a better way to work, you do show him.
You will not be praised, but yelled at you will.
You will yell back, and be fired for that.

When I got out
This is what I should have been told
You will be riddled with "a job why can't you keep."
You will be hounded "a better job can't you get."
You will be compared with those who never served!

When I got out
This is what I should have been told
Names you will be called and mean they will be
To you they will say, "Mother Raper and Baby Killer."
You will be called strange, by those you do not know.
You will be called "crazed" from behind your back.

When I got out
This is what I should have been told
Others will be warned, from you to stay clear.
Others will say, "Watch out for him,"
So quickly he changes, and for that you should fear.

When I got out
This is what I should have been told
Advice you will be given, by those you don't know

Forget where you've been,
And get on with your life.

When I got out
This is what I should have been told
Watch your behind, because you're no longer protected.
Watch your back,
Because others will take your job, try to make you lose.
Watch your back, because sabotaged you will be.

When I got out
This is what I should have been told
You will be quiet, and not say you're a vet.
To yourself you will keep, not knowing other vets.

When I got out
This is what I should have been told
You will not like groups, nor people at all.
You will be lonely, and abandoned by all.

When I got out
This is what I should have been told
Nightmares you will have, in cold sweats you will wake.
You'll not sleep soundly, but quickly you'll wake.
You will shed tears,
By the gallons they will spring forth.
You will not feel right, and not know why.

When I got out
This is what I should have been told
If you marry, divorced you will be.
If you are married, divorced you might be.
You will be hounded,
By the threat of divorce.

When I got out
This is what I should have been told
You will ache and pain, and hurt all inside.
Then one day you will think of ending it all!

When I got out
This is what I should have been told
For years you will suffer, and not know why,
An emotional wreck you will become,
Then you will find a disorder you have!
Then you will find, you're not alone,
There are others who have been through the same!

A Great American Hero

This poem is dedicated to Tom Parker and all who were wounded in action. All of those wounded in action are great American Heroes. They served their country faithfully during the Viet Nam War.

A powerful man was he, the strength of two had he.
Eyes he had, far distant things he could see.
Powerful legs he had, a mighty man was he.

A proud uniform he wore.
Then you found him in war.
Then he carried the burdens of more,
And protected his men in that war.
Because of that more medals he wore.

Then one day, that mighty man he fell,
He was wounded in action, as he fell.

CHARLIE PETERS

On the cold ground he lay
But there he did not stay,
That mighty man's men carried him away.

That day that mighty man left his blood on the ground.
That day, that mighty man, his life he almost gave,
So others he might save.

Torn to shreds, with only one eye to see,
Unable to move, for wounded was he.
Lead in his head, and lead in his back.
But, still was a mighty man was he

For months he lay wounded in bed,
For years he was stitched back together.
Now that man, more mighty than before,
Is a hero, after the war.
No claim to fame, but a hero all the same!

Where I Have Been, I Have Not Been at All

Where I have been, you dare not go, it's a place you never want to have been.
You have been told no one there has been.
Yet, I was there, but it will all be denied, that there I have been.

Where I have been, you cannot go.
Where I have been, you would not want to go.
Where I have been, people are told there I did not go.

Just ask those who sent me there
And they will all say no one has ever been there.
And most likely they can prove no one was there.

Where I have been, no one has ever been.
There is no proof I have been where I have been.
All in authority will deny that I have been where I have been?

But, I was there because I can describe all that is there!
I can tell you all about where I have been and what is there.
If I can describe it so well, how can it be said, "I was not there?"

If I can remember it so well, how can it be said that I was not there at all?
If I can remember it so well, how can it be denied that I was there at all?
If I can describe it so well, how can it ever be said I was not there at all?

There are those that will tell you, with so convincing their words and all,
That where I have been, I have not been there at all.
That where I have been, I was not there at all.

So in the end I have the memories, so vivid they are,
Of where I have been, and yes, I was there after all.
No matter who says that where I have been, I have not been there at all.
But, I was there and can't prove it to any at all.

Homeless

This poem is dedicated to all those that are homeless. Why do people become homeless? There are as many reasons as there are homeless people! We say, "I would never be homeless." But, in all honesty how far away from homelessness are any of us? What calamity in our lives would change our circumstances such that we became homeless? In fact, would it take a calamity or just a minor setback? How long could we be without a job before we became homeless?

When you see a homeless man, you see a man that is begging.
I see a man that is still trying to make a living!

When you see a homeless man, you see a man that is in raggedy clothes.
I see a man that is still able to dress himself!

When you see a homeless man, you see a man that is wearing torn shoes.
I see a man that is still able to tie his shoe laces!

When you see a homeless man, you see a man that has un-kept hair.
I see a man that still has hair!

When you see a homeless man, you see a man holding his hand out.
I see a man that can still use his hand!

When you see a homeless man,
You see a man and wonder how can he live like that?
I see a man that is still living!

When you see a homeless man, you see a man that is down.
I see a man that is trying to get up!

When you see a homeless man, you see a man that is homeless.
I just see a man!

When you see a homeless man,
You wonder how could he allow that to happen.
I wonder how long will it be before I am like him?

When you see a homeless man, you see a man that knows he has problems.
When a homeless man sees you,
He sees a man that doesn't know he has problems!

Hope

A few sentences on pages 90 and 91 of the book "SOLDIER'S HEART: SURVIVORS' VIEW OF COMBAT TRAUMA" caught my eye and deep attention. Those comments are as follows: "... the sense of despair can deepen as veterans relive the past and touch what they see as lost hopes and shattered dreams. They view themselves as 'broken'... But a man or a woman can only despair if he or she has once known hope, had aspirations, or felt a personal peace with the world with his- or herself. It is the loss of hope, the sense that things will never be the same, and that peace is beyond their control that leads to despair... the vets' challenge is to learn who they are, rediscover the sense of hope they once knew, and find peace." In my personal case I view myself as having died on June 20, 1969; the day I entered the military. Though I was drafted, and my induction date was June 24, 1969, I chose to enlist in the Navy. If I would not have been drafted, I would never have enlisted in the Navy.

Before I was drafted my life was filled with goals, dreams, and aspirations, as was the case with all who were drafted! I was working my way through college through part-time jobs and an athletic scholarship. I was a college gymnast and had the hope of competing in the 1972 Olympiad. It was a real hope and one that I was diligently working hard to accomplish. There will always be those that will say that I never would have made it, but, there were also those that said I would never get as far as I did. My future looked very bright, athletics was good and I had a job that was leading to a career. I was finishing my third year at the University of Washington when I received my draft notice. That draft notice shattered everything. After I was discharged I thought I would be able to pick up my life where I had left off, before I was drafted, except for athletics. Nothing could have been further from the truth. I not only was not able to pick up where I had left off, I had to completely start over, from the very bottom. Since being discharged it has been a struggle just to survive, I sometimes wonder how I have gotten as far as I have. What I am now is nothing compared to what I once was. I am a different person that is now just looking to survive. This poem is about the memory I have of what I once was and the hopes I once had. I am very proud of who I once was and very disappointed in what I actually am. I am only a shell of my former self!

Life was so good, and the hopes were so strong,
The harder I worked, the more I could do,
The harder I worked, the more I found I did do.

Life was so good, and the hopes were so strong.
I was starting to realize, the dreams could come true.
The dreams I did have were actually coming true.

Wherever I turned, the doors were not closed,
Everything was opened, and nothing at all closed.
I had control and my future was bright.

I could do no wrong, and there were people to help.
Everything was going my way, nothing could go wrong.
Everywhere I turned, a helping hand was there.

My accomplishments were growing, and more would surely come.
wards were starting to come, to back up my dreams.
Life was so good, and friends there were too.

Everything was lining up; all my ducks were in a row,
I was so proud and respected by all,
I was on my way to a life above them all.

Heartaches were few, but blessings there were a many.
What could go wrong, to this man that was starting to have it all?
All the good things were now coming my way.

All that was left, was for me to stay true to myself,
And stick to the course, that was so clear to myself.
Everything was possible, for this man bettering himself.

Life was so good, no bad days did I have,
The future was bright, with goals now in sight.
All that I dreamed, I was now starting to glean.

Life was so good, and so bright for me at last.
All the hard work, was beginning to pay off.
Life was so good, and I was becoming the best.

No cares did I have, no worries at all
Everything was good with a future so bright.
Nothing could go wrong, because everything was so right!

I think of my accomplishment before I was drafted, and I can't even come close to them after I was discharged. The valleys in my life before being drafted were higher than the peaks in my life after being discharged. The greatest disappointment I have faced is the disappointment I have in myself. I never became anything like I once hope to be. My greatest accomplishment in life after being discharged is that I am still alive, if that is an accomplishment. I now wish that I could just enjoy life for one day, like I once enjoyed every day. What is saddest of all is that my story is not mine alone; it is shared by all others that were drafted.

I Am Glad You Came Back

An individual I have never seen or met inspired this poem, but that individual so affected me that I wrote this poem. On June 6, 1994, I called the Mike Reagan radio talk show. The subject was WWII veterans. When I called I first talked with the receptionist and told her my subject was to thank WWII vets for the fine example they set for the following generation. Then she asked me if I was a vet, I said yes. Then she asked if I was a Viet Nam Vet and again I said yes. To which she said "welcome home, I am glad you made it back."

When she said that it hit me, since being discharged from the Navy I had not heard those words. No one, not one person, had said to me "welcome home, I am glad you made it back!" It instantly caused me to burst into tears. I lost complete control for several minutes. All that time she kept saying "I am sorry; I didn't mean to bring up any bad memories." After I finally regain my composure and was able to speak, I explained to her that what she had just said was the very first time I had heard those words or similar words. How good those words made me feel! As a Viet Nam Vet, I was not used to kind words such as that. However, kindness was not something I was accustomed to. Concerning being a Viet Nam Vet, it was unkindness and harsh words I had become accustomed to hearing. Those words "welcome home, I am glad you made it back" on June 7, 1994, the day after the above call was made!

When to war I once did go, a party was given for me,
From my friends that I once did have.
Would they be glad, if I did come back?
Would they be sad, if I did not come back?

When I did come back, would my friends be glad that I was back?
Would they remember that once I was their friend?
Would they say, "I am glad you are back?"

For years I did wait to hear, and not a word was said in my ear!
Then one day those words I did hear,
"I am glad that you came back", to again be here.

What those words "I am glad you came back" did mean to me.
That someone was glad, to have me return.
That someone was glad that I did not die over there.
That someone was glad, to have me back over here.
That someone was glad and cared about me.

I was glad to know, that someone cared about me.
I was glad to know, that someone remembered me.

I was glad to know, that someone cared and knew,
That what I gave up, when I went over there,
Would never be replaced, when I came back over here.

I was glad to know that someone remembered,
That liberty and freedom I gave up,
So that they would not have theirs to give up.

I was glad to know that they remembered
That I gave up the life I once could have had,
Only to have the life I would have to accept!

I was glad to know that they remembered,
That I gave up the life I once could have had,
So that they now might have the life they could have.

I was glad to know that they remembered,
That I gave up the dreams I did have,
And knew they would only be dreams I would dream of having.

I was glad to know that they remembered,
That in my prime I did give to my country,
So that they in their prime, could have from their country.

I was glad to know that someone cared enough
To say, "I am glad you came back"
And you are now here to stay.
I was glad to know, that someone cared about me,
And then said to me "I am glad you came back."

Thank you for caring and saying to me,
"I am glad you came back", meaning to me,
That "I am glad you're alive and did not die."
"I am glad you came back", meaning to me,
That freedom and liberty you fought for me,
You can now enjoy right along with me.

Because someone said, "I am glad you came back,"
Now, I have come back, I have really come back,
Because you said to me "Welcome back"
And "I am glad you have come back."

Now, to all Vets that served their country so well,
Welcome home, I am glad you came back.
I am glad you survived, and I am glad you are alive!

I Know What It's Like

I know what it's like, to have to forget.
To forget those behind and my past that's with them,
To have to forget, so I can survive right now.

I know what it's like to have to fight like a man,
When you would rather be playing like a boy.
I know what it's like to have to think like a man,
When all I've been is a boy all my life.

I know what it's like, to have to lay still.
No moves can I make, so I will not be found,
So quiet I must be while I am waiting,
No moves dare I make and I have to lay as still as I can.

I know what it's like, on others to depend.
I know what it's like when there's no place to hide.
I know what it's like when there's no place to run.

I know what it's like to go without sleep for days upon end.
I know what it's like to go without food and water and have to fight to the
end.
I know what it's like to not think about self,
But think about buddies clear to the end.

I know what it's like to be all alone and no comfort receive.
I know what it's like for no shelter to receive.
I know what it's like to hope the last rites I'll receive.

I know what it's like to pray for the end.
I know what it's like to not be able to pray for the end.
I know what it's like to hope there is no end.

I know what it's like to be frightened to death
And still have to fight or lose my life.
I know what it's like to have to do, what I've been told is wrong all my life.
I know what it's like, not to know what to do with my life.

I know what it's like to wake with cold sweats and shakes.
I know what it's like to wake from my scream and to be woken with a shake.
I know what it's like to not know what's wrong with my life.

I Want to Go Home

I want to go home, I want to go home, oh, how I want to go home.
I remember a place, a place where I've been, a place I once called home.
So nice it was, to be in that place, how safe it was being back home.
I remember it well, and it was swell, that place I've often called my home.

Away from home I am, so far away I am, oh, how I don't like being away.
Away from those I love, away from those I miss,
Oh, how I miss home and being away.
I want to go back, and get away from here,
Oh, how I need rest from it all and just get away.
I need to get away; I need to go back, Oh, I want from here to get away.

Why am I here, fighting in this land?
Oh, how I want to get out of here and away from this land.
This is no place to be, I want to go home,
Oh, how I want to get out of this land.
Why did I leave, why did I go,
Oh, was it just to fight in a war that's far away land?

I wasn't raised a fighter, I wasn't raised a killer,
Oh, how I want that peace that's not in this land.

The losses are great, the losses are high,
And each day we're here they mount ever higher.
I never did know that war was so bad; oh, it's a tragedy to have to go to war.
I don't like what I do; I don't like what I see,
Oh, how sometimes I even I hate what I think over here.
I want to get out of here, and never come back,
I never want to return back over here.

Away from home base, it's not very safe,
Oh, how it frightens me to death being in this place.
To know I'm in a place, where there's no place to run,
Oh, how at times I need to run and hide some place.
Some days I often think, it's the worst it can get,
And again I learn I was wrong about this place.
The next day is worse, far worse than before,
Oh, how it eats away at me being in this place.

Each day I fight, I know I might not last,
Oh, how I know I might not live and this day might be my last.
Yesterday I thought, in the battle I fought,
Oh, how I thought it was going to be my last.
In the middle of battle, when the pressures to great,
All I can think of is fighting my best.
For you dare not think, of anything else,
Or surely you'll be carried away to your final rest.

I don't want to be, in this place over here, Oh, how very bad it is way over here.
It's so frightful to see, what happens over here,
Oh, how I hate being in this place over here.
You have to fight the foe, till their blown away,
You have to react to what's all around over here.
If I move real fast, then I might last,
When it's all done I can shed my tears and wipe them clear.

When the fighting over, that's when I think,
Oh, how I want to go home and get away from here.
I can't imagine now, how old I've become,
Because of fighting in a war that's way over here.
It's hard to believe, a kid I used to be, before I was brought over here.
But, when I relax, I remember being a kid,
And being back home so far away from here.

I want to see someone, I knew from the past,
Oh, how I'd like to see anyone that's from back home.
I'd like to hear their voices, I'd like to talk to them,
Oh, just to see someone that's from back home.
It's lonely over here, I want to go home,
Oh, how once again I want to be back home.
I'm all by myself, there's no one to tell,
Alone I am and all by myself, here away from home.

I can't let anyone know, the way I feel inside,
Oh, how I must hide that I miss it back home.
Home is where I want to be, home is where I'd like to be,
Oh, how I really miss being back home.

I must put up a face, a face that's very strong,
A face that hides what I really feel inside.
No one must know, how alone I really feel,
Sick it makes being alone over here and away from home.

It drives me crazy, to see what I do, oh, how I think I'll lose my mind.
There's no time to play, and run around at night,
Oh, how I just want to live through another night.
Why is there war? Why are lives being lost?
Why can't it be like it was back home?
I don't like what I see, I don't like what I do, Oh, how I don't think I'll last.

Now, I have to survive, and live to the end,
So, that means I have to forget about going back home.
I can't think of the past, or surely I won't last,
Oh, I must forget about going back home.
If I remember my past, I know I won't last, Oh, now I must forget my past.
If I do last, I can get out of here,
And then I'll go back home and maybe live in my past.

It's hard to believe, what you really have to do, just to survive and stay alive.
It's driving me insane, being over here, and missing all that's back home.
I don't like being here. I hate what I do. Oh, how I hate all I have to do.
When I'm all by myself,
It's hard for me to believe, how this war has changed me so much.

All I want to do is get out of here, and finally go home and be out of here.
I want to forget, this whole big mess,
Oh, how I want to go back home and get out of here.

Once I get home, maybe I can forget, all I had to do while I was over here.
Once I get home, I think I'll be safe,
And my life can be like it was once I'm away from here.

There's too much to do, just to survive,
So, I've got to forget about going back home so I can survive.
I have to forget, what I left behind,
Oh, now I must forget about going back home just to stay alive.
I try to forget, my home in the past,
And continue to fight so I can be one that will last and survive.
If I want to see home, that home in my past, then,
I have to forget about going back there.

When it gets real bad, it tears me apart, and I wonder how long I'll last.
Sometimes I think the worst, and the end is very near,
Oh, how I wonder if it's finally my end.
I don't want to go,
But, when it's my time, then there's no way I'll last to go back home.
I don't want to go. I want to live till the end. Oh, how I want to go home.

Now I have to live, in this land over here,
And now think of it as home away from home.
I have to make the best, of this place over here,
And hope I can truly last and rest back at home.
If I can survive, and return back home,
Then I will again see those I left behind back at home.
But to see those left behind, then I have to forget,
Forget all that's back at my home.

But, how can I forget, the home that I left,
When, all I really want is to go home.
Try as I may, try as I might, I still can't forget about my home.
I still want to go, back to my home, oh, how I want to go home.
The memories are strong, of all that's back home,
It's hard to forget what I once called home.

It's hard not to think of where I came from. Oh, how I want to go home.
I remember it well, of the home where I'm from, Oh, how I want to go home.
It was peaceful back there, in the place I am from, Oh, how I want to go home.
I can't stop missing the place I am from. Oh, how I want to go home.

The longer I'm here, the more my memory fades,
Oh, how sad it would be to finally forget.
To finally forget, about life back home. But, how long can my memory last.
Of that place I once knew, the place I call home, Oh, how I still want to go
home.
I want to go home, before I finally forget,
And home just becomes a place I once lived.

I'm afraid before long, I'll forget about home, if I'm here just a little too long.
It's so long ago now, I've almost forgotten home, now, I've been here too long.
I'm now getting so close, but afraid I won't last,
Oh, how I want to make it back home.
I really want to last, to make it back home, Oh, how I want to go home.

No matter how hard I try, and how hard I fight,
I still can't forget about going back home.
The desire is still strong, and the thoughts still last,

About going back home, the home in my past.
I can never forget, never really forget, about going back home,
The place I can't forget.
When all seems lost, there's one thing that's not gone,
And that's the hope of finally going back home.

I woke up one day, and decided myself, Oh, how I wanted to go home.
The desire is so strong, to finally go home,
Sometimes I'd like to forget why I have to be away from home.
I really can't forget, about the place I call home,
I really do just want to go back home.
I want to go home; I want to go home,
Oh, how I really want to go home.

Jobs

Before entering the military, during the Viet Nam War, jobs were plentiful. There were always summer jobs, part time jobs, temporary jobs and full time jobs. After graduating from high school some went on to college and others found work that eventually led to a career. Many were able to find work in areas that they enjoyed. Most looked forward to working for one company, until they retired. All, of course, entered the job market at entry level positions, which led to other positions and a career. Many, upon entering the military, had passed the entry level positions and were on their way to a career. Then came the military, some drafted, others enlisted; they left their jobs. However, after leaving the military, they did not enter the job market where they would have been, had they not been in the military. Neither did they re-enter the job market where they left off, when going into the military. They had to start over and accept entry level positions. Here is an example.

I was discharged from the Navy in San Diego, CA, in 1975. I could *not get an engineering job there. The only job I could get was as a Security Guard, starting at $2.00/hour. That was hardly enough to support a wife and 4 children. I moved back to Seattle, my home of record. Before going into the Navy, I worked as an Engineering Aid for the City of Seattle Engineering Department, Traffic Division.*

We got back to Seattle, settled into a house, and I went down to the Seattle Municipal Building—up to the 4th floor to get my old job back. A manager came up to the counter where I was standing and started questioning me; he didn't even invite me into his office so we could talk privately. He was curious as to what I wanted. I told him I worked for the Traffic Division when I received my Draft Notice, and I understand I can get my old job back. I showed him my Draft Notice and my DD214. He looked at both. Then he said to me, with a straight face, and I can still hear those words echoing in my mind, "We don't have to hire you back!"

I replied, "I thought Congress passed a law that stipulated that if I was drafted, the company I worked for had to give me my old job back."

He said, without even taking a breath, "That is true. However, you were in more than four years. So, we don't have to hire you back, and we do not have any job openings that you can fill." Wow, talk about cutting clear to my heart. I was dumbfounded but kept my composure. He shook my hand and said, "Good luck in finding a job."

To this day I don't know if he was sincere or being sarcastic! I thanked him. He then turned away and walked back to his office. I, on the other hand, turned around and walked away. I thought to myself, when I reached the street, "Well, what a mistake that was coming back to Seattle to get my old job back." I couldn't help but remember that was the same company who six years ago would have paid me to get my master's degree and let me drive a city car to attend classes; all I had to give them was five more years of working for the city. My, oh my, I sure lost my value in six years, and I thought the city really liked me! Now, my full-time job will be looking for a job.

This poem was written to describe jobs and being laid off after the military.

Jobs, jobs, jobs, we all wanted jobs.
At first the one we had before,
But, no, they didn't have to hire us,
Just because we worked for them before.

Then it was one like the one we had before,
But, no, no recent experience did we have,
No references or resume did we have.

Then it was to try to get a job we thought we would like to have.
But, no, they didn't hire us, no experience did we have.
Then it was to try to get a job, any job was acceptable.
It proved not to be this or that,
But rather, the first one who hired us.

The excuses were a plenty that we heard,
Not qualified it seems that you are,
Overqualified it appears you are,
No experience do you have.

The excuses kept growing at an alarming rate,
We just filled that position, you are too late.
We have decided no need to fill that position.
More people we do have to interview.

We will call you, if an opening does arise.
If we find we need someone with your qualifications,
You we will surely call.

We will keep you on file, just in case.
We will call you, don't call us!

The Day I Met John

A bus ride to town started my day.
A quite ride seemed what it would be, on that day.
No was one speaking and all were deep within their own thoughts,
on that day.

A few stops later, John stepped on the bus,
And all could see he was not like the rest of us.
Obvious at first glance, John would not let this ride normal be,
For the rest of us.
His appearance was un-kept and unshaven;
Some may have thought he was homeless, unlike us.

Boisterous he would prove to be and reminisce about the past he did have.
Still drunk from the night before, and now looking to start it again.
His words from subject to subject they appeared to wander.

From Richard Millhouse Nixon he started
And to the Mekong Delta he did go.

Many thought he was rambling on about nothing at all
And they wanted him to go.
However, it did not take long to ascertain that in Vietnam he once had to go.

To society John is looked down on,
And somewhere else is where they would rather have him be.
Most have forgotten the war John once fought,
But John has not forgotten what used to be!
He has not forgotten, nor will he ever forget the war he fought in,
So long ago and where he used to be.

Most ignore that where John is today, is a result of where he was in a war.
Most cannot realize what John gave up, when he was asked to fight in a war.
Most cannot understand what John went through,
When he was asked to fight in a war.

Most cannot imagine what John saw then and still sees today.
Most choose to ignore, that John would not be what he is today,
If he had not been asked to fight in that war,
So long ago, but to him it is only yesterday.

Most would like to ignore the bad side that war brings for some and for all.
Most have forgotten John was once a man that was respected by all.
But, because of what he is today, he is not liked by any at all.

For me, I wondered how far am I really from being like what John is today?
How easy would it be for me to become like John
And be detested by all today?

As I stepped off the bus I couldn't help but think
"Now, I have to be normal, to be accepted today."

I can't help but think how normal are John and I and why?
How much different are John and I and why?
Society accepts one of us, but not the other, why?

But, does society really accept either one of us, or are we both just looked at?
Many looked at John and wondered, "How could he become like that?"
I looked at John and wondered,
"Why did I not become like John and be like that?"

If I Would Have

If I would have died, before I went to war,
So many are the numbers, which would have been there in the end.

So many to pay their last respects,
So many that would have said,
Such a great loss it is
To have his life cut so short.

So many lives he touched,
In the short time he was here.
He will be sorely missed,
And forever be remembered.

But, I did not die in a war over there.
And if I should die today,
So few are the numbers that would be there at my side.

Now all they could say would be
Here lies a man, who lived a full life,
He has loved ones that will miss him,
And that is about all.

I Was Not

This poem may be applied to many, many who have lost their identity. That identity may have been lost, or taken away, for many reasons, some of which could be: the military, being raped, accident which limited their physical appearance or abilities, discrimination (whatever ugly form it has), to name a few. There are actually thousands of others reasons, which a person's identity may be lost or changed.

I once knew who I thought I was,
But, who I thought I was, is not who I really was.
Who I never was, is who I actually was,
And who I was, I never knew I really was.

Now, that I know who I really am,
I wonder who it was that I thought I was,
I wonder who it was that others thought I was?

Now, that I know who I really am,
I wonder why those who knew who I really was,
Never let me know who I really was?

Why did those who knew who I really was,
Make me think I was who I was not,
And not let me know who I really was?

What I became, I became because of who I was not.
And, what I could have become, I never became,
Because, I was not allowed to become who I really was.

The person I became, was not the real person I was,
But, it was the person I was not.
The person I didn't become, was the person I really was,
And didn't know that was the person I was.

Now, I wonder who I really am,
Am I the person I never was?
Or, am I not the person I thought I was?

The person I am is not the person I really am.
And the person I am not is the person I really am.
Am I the person I am not, or am I not the person I am?

Laid Off

Companies come and companies go,
But while they are here, they do hire and fire.
When you are not in need, it is layoff time indeed.
The excuses are many, and sometimes it is just plain greedy.

"Times are slow right now, so we are going to have to let you go."
"We did not get the contracts that we thought would be ours."
"We lost the bids and so some have to go."

"You have been a big help and we are glad you were here.
But, there are just too many that still work here."

These are the things said, but more is implied.
"You are very good, but too good compared to the rest."
"You work hard, so hard the others complain."
"You know a lot, but frankly you just know too much."

"We have paid you too much,
And now have found someone to work not for so much."
"You have learned well and now I am afraid my job you will have."
"You are too old to keep up with the rest."

Life

Life is a gift that all should appreciate. When times are good, it is greatly appreciated. But, when times get bad, it is something that is so easily forgotten. When times aren't good, we may think of a final solution. It is a permanent solution to a temporary problem. Though temporary the problem may be, at the time it may not be a temporary problem to us. The following is a poem about some things to remember, when the times aren't so good and we may be thinking about ways to permanently solve the problem.

Life, what's it all about?
What is its meaning?
When we are young, we do not think about it.
We play, are curious, and learn many new things.

As we grow older,
We see distant relatives, great aunts and uncles, die.
There is still no meaning to life,

We didn't really know them,
They were just people that others knew.

Then as we continue to grow older,
Ones we really know begin to die,
A grandparent, an aunt, an uncle, a friend.

As the years go by, we see this number increase,
As this number increases,
So does the loss, the emptiness and hurt.

Now we begin to think, what is life all about?
We see great sorrow and sadness
When these dearly loved one depart.
We feel the loss and emptiness when they are absent.

Then as we continue to grow older,
Closer ones die, a parent, a brother, a sister, a close friend.
The hurt becomes greater.

We then remember all the others who have departed before.
And the pain grows even more.
We remember all the things

We wish we would have done and said.
Too late, we feel worse.
The memories linger,
Oh, if I would have only???
The pain grows, why didn't I???

We ponder and wonder about life,
Still the pain grows.
We ask why, why now, it's too soon!

I have not done all I wanted to do for you!
How much more can I take?
Who is next, how long will it be?

We begin to wonder,
What is the use, so much hurt and sorrow.
Life starts to get serious.

We have doubts about our own life.
Is it worth it? So much suffering,
I could stop the misery.

But wait; there are those left that love me,
A wife, husband, daughter, son, grandchild, friend,
If I should depart I would cause them
The same pain and misery that I am suffering.

I don't want them to suffer,
I want them to be happy.
You know, they need me, they love me, they want me.

Now life takes on new meaning.
I need to let those left know I love them.

I need to tell them
Those things I wish I would have told others.

I need to help them, love them,
Be there for them.
The loss, the emptiness, the hurt
Is replaced by those left.

So life, though it has pain, suffering and misery,
Is worth living.
I will think of others,
I will go on, life is worth living.

I am needed and loved,
So let me help and love those left.
I will think of others and not myself.
I will now live life and enjoy it.

Looking

Always looking at what's around,
Always looking to see what lays ahead.
Always looking to see what falls behind.

Always looking to my left and to my right.
Always looking to see what's at my side.
Always looking at what's up overhead.

Always looking at what's down below.
Always looking to see what's out there.
Always peering to see what way is beyond.

Always looking for what's supposed to be there,
Always looking for what should not be there.
Always looking for what's out of place.

How nice it would be to not have to look anymore.

How nice it would be to not have to look out there.

How nice it would be to only have to see what is really there.

The Lottery

From 1969 through 1973 the draft was based on a lottery system. All those between 18 and 26 were in that lottery. It was called the draft lottery. Three hundred sixty-six numbers were placed in a bin, each representing a day of the year, the birth day of all those who were in that lottery. Then numbers were drawn at random. I was born on November 6 and my lottery number was number 47, the first year it was played. Six months prior to that lottery drawing I had already been drafted.

In 1969 a new game was to be played, it was a draft lottery.
The government of the young, did run this lottery,
They set the rules, which had to be obeyed.
Only those young, were allowed to play this lottery.

The rules of the game, were simple at that,
Young was defined as between twenty-six and eighteen.

All those older had beaten the draft,
All those younger would get their chance to play.

What happened to youth, was set by a number,
There were 366 numbers to be drawn,
Representing the birth days of the youth,
No chance to escape, all had to play.

Surely would go all whose number was early drawn,
Others would stay, whose numbers were later drawn
All were anxious; to see which number they had drawn
Those were the saddest, whose numbers were first drawn.

Those drawn last, thought they were safe at last.
Those in between hoped for the best,
Hoped they might not be called,
But knew they might go.

For one day year, all youths lives hung on a limb,
Hoping that their number was last,
Hoping all others would have their number first.

When numbers were drawn, for some to their relief,
And for others it was a frown of grief.
For some their stomachs did churn,
Because they did realize it was now their turn.

All numbers were drawn,
Some that were drawn, would lead to war,
Others that were drawn would be far away from war.

Love

As I look back over my years
One thing I have learned
Is that love is greatest
The greatest of all.

To love and be loved
No greater thing can be had.
How wonderful it is
To love and be loved.

Love helps to endure the times,
No matter how troublesome they may seem to be.

To love and be loved,
Means someone to share with
Life and all that may come.

Someone to cry with, through those troublesome times.
Someone to laugh with, through the happiest of times.
Someone to share, the dreams you hope to be.
Someone to care, for your deepest emotions and thoughts.

Someone to hear, your stories of woe.
Someone to listen, when you speak from your heart.
Someone to say, when you are troubled at heart,
You are going to be fine, and all will be well.

Someone to comfort, when things hurt so much.
Someone to praise, for just being around.
Someone to fill that void, so deep, wide and broad.
Someone to be with, to be with for all time to come.

My Fair Indian Maiden

This poem was inspired by Kevin Costner's movie "Dances with Wolves" and my love of the outdoors.

My fair Indian Maiden, so fair you are.
Graceful as bounding antelope
Swiftly moving across the plains.

My fair Indian Maiden, beautiful you are,
More beautiful than blossoming meadows in spring time,
Even fresh flowers can't compare.
Breath taking you are,
More than the majestic morning sun
Rising above the hills.

The sparkle in your eye,
Is as the twinkling of the starry heavens at night.

The beauty of the stare of your eyes,
Surpasses even the beauty of moon beams at night.

Your smile radiates friendliness and care,
As a fresh flower radiating beauty.
Your pleasant, sweet, soft voice,
More pleasant to hear than
The rain gently dropping on the forest floor,
Or streams gently moving through their banks.

The singing in your voice,
Not even chirping of birds can compare.

The sweetness of your kiss,
More desirable it is,
Than the most delicious nectar
From the sweetest of fruits.

My fair Indian Maiden,
Even your tender touch,
Oh, so soft and gentle it is,
More gentle and refreshing
Than even the gentle evening breeze.

The warmth of your breasts against my bosom,
Warmer than the midday sun beating down on my chest.
So fresh you are,
Fresh as the morning frost.
Skin so soft and fair, you have,

Soft as fresh flower petals,
Such natural beauty,
Even the heavens above can't compare.

So caring you are,
Such caring even the animals don't share.
Such playfulness you display,
Greater than that of a young fawn
Frolicking through the woods.

Such power you have,
Not even a raging river can compare.
So protective you are, even a nursing sow can't compare.

Your stature, more stout than the tallest of redwoods.
Such industrious you display,
Even the beaver can't compare.

Such vision you have,
Even eagles can't compare.
So wise you are, even the night owl can't compare.

My fair Indian Maiden,
Gentle as a quietly moving stream you are.

My fair Indian Maiden,
As high as the mountain peaks,
I am, when I am with you.

My fair Indian Maiden,
Most desirable of them all you are.

So, my fair Indian Maiden,
You are by far the fairest of them all.

Man Down Over Here

This poem is dedicated to David Forest Gutowski and all Navy Corpsman. Dave was a Navy Corpsman during the Viet Nam War. He was attached to a Marine Squad. Often he found himself in the bush with that squad. He died May 6, 1996. He was in need of medical attention but preferred death to medical attention. As Dave told me, while he was alive, not a night went by that he didn't have nightmares. He also said that he had not gotten a sound night's sleep since the war! There won't be any flags at half-mast for Dave, except for the half-mast in the hearts of those who knew him and the one that was at half-mast outside the Mortuary. Dave's reward for serving his country well and saving the lives of others during war was the Veteran's Administration helping to pay for a head stone and giving a flag to a close friend of his. The U.S. Navy did provide an Honor Guard, but there was no twenty-one-gun salute for this fine G.I. who put his life on the line to save the lives of others. What is truly sad is that some who ran during the Viet Nam War and dodged the draft can now get a fine military burial, with

Honor Guard, twenty-one-gun salute, and all the flags flying in the country at half-mast. But, for Dave, who didn't run but fought, just a head stone and a flag. It's ironic, glory for those that ran, and nothing for those who fought!

Dave's death was hard on me because I was making a special shotgun stock for him, which would allow him to shoot right-handed, while using his left eye to sight with. We called it the cross-eyed stock. It was not finished in time for him to see that special stock. Never did I imagine that he would pass away before I finished the stock. I wish I had finished it sooner so that he could have used his shotgun the way he wanted to. He was going to get back into shooting competition with that cross-eyed shotgun. Joy to a craftsman is not the making of something; the joy comes in seeing the happiness in those who received the crafted product. I deeply regret not having finished it for him to see and to use!

This poem is also dedicated to 'Doc' Willie 'Fat Quack' McCrite and all Navy Corpsman who have served and are serving and will serve on U.S. Submarines. All Corpsman are greatly loved and respected by all those they serve with. They all go above and beyond the call of duty to save the life of their comrades. It was a sad day when 'Doc' McCrite went on Eternal Patrol and he will be greatly missed, but he will never be forgotten.

'Hey, Corpsman, Hey, Corpsman, man down over here.'
Dodging bullets and mortars, to get to that man down over there.
Not a thought of saving his own life, but only that of saving his buddies life,
The life of that man who is down over here.

Ignore the fears and the sounds, to save the soul
Of that man who is now down over there.
That man down over there, a man who is wounded over there,
This time not a causality, because of the corpsman who is right here.

This life now saved, and not a moment to spare, then all of a sudden,
'Hey, Corpsman, Hey, Corpsman, a man down over here.'
More bullets to duck, more mortars to dodge,
To get to that man who is down over there.

This time no luck for that man down over there.
But, there's no time to think, and there's no time to rest,
Because here come those words, again and again,
'Hey, Corpsman, Hey, Corpsman, man down over here.'

After the war, another call is now heard,
'Hey, God, Hey God, man down over here.'
It's a corpsman who gave of himself, to save the life of others.
Please take him and care for him, please find a place for him,
Please find a final resting place for him,
That man who is now right there with you!

Memorial Day

A day set aside to remember the past,
A day set aside to remember those lost,
A day set aside to remember the cost.

On this day all remember the sacrifices so great,
That have been made by heroes and all,
So we might be free to live as we want.

On this day I remember those I knew,
Who gave up their lives so freedom we will always know.
I remember those who sacrificed with their lives,
So that people knew no harm would come to their lives.

On this day I remember the sacrifices of every generation,
Generations that have long passed away,
Generations that are soon to pass away,
And the generation that is now sacrificing.

Try as I might and try with all my soul,
I try not to remember how close I came to offering my sacrifice.
I try not to remember the loud noises so close to my ears.
I try not to remember the high whines that passed me by.

I try not to remember the silence so loud,
I try not to remember the fear that was bound up inside,
I try not to remember the prayer - I thought was my last to make.
I try not to remember the aches and pains that are still fresh in my mind.

No matter how hard I try, I can never forget.
I can never forget how close I came to just being a memory,
And wondering if others would remember my sacrifices and me,
As I remember those who were before me and the giving of their sacrifices.

Memories

There are times that we wish we had taken more time to take care of those things that are most important in our lives. Those most important things are family and friends. I just received a message that a dear family relative is no longer with us and that is a hard pill to swallow. As the years pass by more and more are added to that list. Many, many years ago I wrote a poem about losing family and friends. Here is that poem, titled "Memories." This time I honor my nephew, Chris Dispo, and the memories he left me with.

From times long past,
Come memories of long ago,
Memories that have lasted a lifetime.

Memories that have carried,
Carried me through times both good and bad.
Memories of those who were warm and kind,
Memories of those who were soft and gentle.

Memories of those, who kind words came forth,
Kind words that made soft the harshness around.
Memories of those, whose tender touch,
Once touched my heart.

Memories of those, who cared to share,
To remind us of good that could be everywhere!
Memories of those, I once held dear,
For the memory of them, is still to me very clear.

The memory of them, even dreams cannot compare!
The memory of them has long warmed my heart!
Though the memories of them have been with me long,
I now long to see them, for new memories to share.

I long to see them,
For new memories to make!
It saddens me to now know,
That those fond memories is all I now have left.
Don't hold back any longer in letting others know you care about them.

Military Friends

In the military one quickly learns to make friends. These are called your buddies. You become very close to them. However, as they quickly come, they also quickly go. When you transfer, or they transferred, to a new duty station, one has to let them go. For those that have been in battle, some see their friends go in the blink of an eye.

In my mind it was a short time ago,
That friends we were and it doesn't seem that long ago.
Not for long, did the friendship last
But, the memory of that friendship is not in my past.

I remember that friendship well,
I still laugh at what we laughed at them,
And tears still come to my eyes,
As they did back then.

I remember the joys and sorrows,
I remember the good times we had
I remember the beers we had,
The walls of bottles and cans on the tables we had.

Seize the Moment in Time

Whatever you do
Never forget to seize the moment in time.

Moments in time, so quickly they pass.
Don't let them pass
Without seizing them to see what will be.

Seize the moment in time
And reach for the stars.
Seize the moment in time
To climb the mountains above.

Seize the moment in time
And not regret the thoughts of what could have been.
Seize the moment in time,
To become the best at whatever you can.

Nurses, Angels of Mercy

They were young and full of life,
Hoping they could do some good and help save someone else's life,
Hoping they would make a difference in other's life.

Full of hopes and strong convictions that they had,
They went to war in a faraway land.
Not really knowing what was over there waiting in that far away land?

After arrival in that far away land, that was ravaged with war, which was easy
to see.
They soon learned that it was not the best they would see,
In fact they soon learned it was the worst life had to offer they would see.

They never knew those young men, when the young men were at their best,
When the young men were strong, healthy and in their prime.
They didn't even know who their families back home were.

They knew nothing about those fine young men,
Except what they saw before their eyes,
And what they saw was not what they wanted to see, through their eyes.

They never saw what the loved ones back home
Remembered about those on their back.
They never saw the power those once had, as they lay there on their back.
They never knew the hope those once had, as they lay helpless on their back.

They only saw the worst that could happen to men, those men who were on
their backs.
They saw men who were suffering the most, as they lay there on their backs.
They saw men who didn't even look like men anymore;
They only saw flesh lying on their backs.

They saw the mangled flesh and the torn limbs,
They saw those who would never see again and others who would never walk
again.
And worst of all they saw those who would never love again.

They were even the last that some would see, as their last breath they took while
on their back.
They tried their best to comfort give, to those that were helpless on their back.
They tried their best to smile at them, while their tears for a few moments they
held back.

They tried their best to be a ray of hope, to those mangled men who lay on their
backs.
Consoling words they often said, to any and all who lay there on their backs.

Sometimes knowing they were the last words the young man would hear, while he lay on his back.

Many a hand they did hold, as the wounded lay on their back.
Many heads they did stroke, as the wounded lay on their back.
With the gentleness that made many see Angel's above them, while they lay on their back.

To many a young man they said "I love you" and you will make it back home.
But, they knew they had to speak fast, for the young man was not long to last,
They did that so the young man would finally have comfort at last.

Many a young man's hand went limp, while they were holding it in theirs.
Many a young man's eyes turned glossy, while they were staring at them.
Many lips they saw quiver, as the last breath rolled out of his mouth.

All they could think was this was some mother's young son,
This was someone's brother and somebody else's lover.
This was some fathers pride and joy, who was now on his back.

Many they thought they lost, always thinking I should have done more.
Many they thought they lost, always thinking I should have said more.
Many they thought they lost, always thinking if only I would have been faster and done more.

What many did not know was they were Angel's of Mercy sent from above,
To those who lay there on their back and looking at those who were above.
And to those there on their backs, those nurses were truly Angel's sent from above.

To many on their backs, theirs was the last smile they saw.
To many on their backs, theirs were the last words they heard.
To many on their backs, theirs were the last touch they felt.

What those Angel's sent from above, may have forgot was that to those on their back,
It was their smile, words and touch that finally brought them back.
Those Angel's sent from above did what no other could possibly do and they never fell back.

Their smile, words and touch, saved many a life,
So they could go home at last and live the rest of their life.
Those young men never forgot those Angel's sent from above
And felt they had saved their life.

Those young men long remember the glow of that face, from those Angel above,
Those young men never forgot the songs,
Which were sung by those Angel's above.
Those young men always remembered the words,
From those Angel's above.

Yes, they were Angels of Mercy sent from above,
To those young men who lay on their backs, and looking at them who were above
Men who would have been helpless and hopeless, without those Angel's sent from above.

Yes, they were Angel's sent from above, who were willing to pay the cost.

Without those Angel's sent from above, more would have been lost,

Both during and after that war, when their hope they would have otherwise lost.

Occupied Space

The passing away of a dear loved one.

There once was a time when I occupied no space,
And there was no memory of me, for I was yet to be.
Then suddenly I came into being, and then space I started occupying,
It was in the here and now, and for how long I did not know.

For a lifetime I lived, in that space I occupied.
I gathered things around me, both visible and not.
◻I willingly shared that space I occupied, with you and many more.
Together we shared that space that was ours.

While in the space I once occupied
An impression I left, which is now remembered by others.
Then, suddenly, I no longer occupied that space any more behind.

The space I once occupied can no longer be seen.
It can only be felt and remembered,
Within the space of other's minds, with the memories I left behind.

When I stopped occupying that space, which I once called my own,
Is now the space I left behind, in other people's minds,
We do leave behind that which is most important in life,
And that is the memories we leave in other people's mind.

It is hard to accept the death of those we love,
Unless we accept the love they left behind.
The love that can never be taken away,
Even though the space they once occupied is no longer there.

We are not gone,
As long as we are in the memories of those we knew and loved.
I left behind all my love for others, in the space I once occupied for myself.

For those that still occupy space, where I once did myself,
Never let go of the love I left behind.
Remember my love well, while you still occupy space, which I left behind.
Never let go of the love that was there but remember it well.

Remember the love of all those who once occupied space,
Remember the love they left behind,
And not the sorrow of the space they once occupied,
That space they once occupied is now part of the space you still occupy.

I now occupy space in a place
Where pain is gone and suffering is no more,
In a place where all tears have been wiped away,
In a place where grief is no more, and crying is gone from all faces,
It is a place where pain of heart plagues no one at all in the new space I now
occupy.

My space in the here and now is now gone,
But the memory of me is still there for all to enjoy!
The space I once occupied,
Has now been freed up for others to occupy.

Ode To Vets Returning

Two times a year I try to post veteran poetry. It did not matter where returning vets served or in what capacity. During the 1960s & '70s, they were all lumped together when they were discharged and became the scourge of America. Here are some comments that were directed toward me, some even years after I was discharged.

A workmate said to me, "You Baby Killer and Mother Raper."

Another workmate piped up, "What you vets need to do is forget where you were and get on with your lives!"

A different workmate yelled out to me, "Hey, aren't you a vet? " I replied yes, and he said, "Oh, that explains everything!"

A WWII vet (the pride of America, right?) told me, "You Viet Nam vets are nothing but a bunch of crybabies!"

There are more derogatory and insulting comments that have been made to vets, but that should get my point across. One thing returning vets quickly learned was not to retaliate, but to "just grin and bear it." More Vietnam vets committed suicide after they were discharged than were "Killed in Action." This poem is for those that suffered much after returning.

Off to war they went,
Leaving family, friends, wives, lovers and more.
Young and innocent they were.
Returning they hoped, dying they might.
Forgotten they became, unwanted they thought,
While they were off to war.

Returning they did, standing or laying they arrived.
Those standing thought they were safe.
Home they were, safe and secure?
But to the home they returned,
It was not the home they had left!
It was not the same as it was before,
The place they came back to was just not the same anymore.

For many, it was hard to leave,
But even harder to return.
For many, tears they did shed,
For wives and lovers, they now had none.
Because they had left them for others,
And left them all alone.

Hard it became, because work there was none.
Hire a vet was the saying heard loud and clear,
But country and men, wanted those that had stayed,
Not those that had gone.
A chance to succeed was not given them.
When they returned, a second chance to succeed,
Was not given them.

Friends they had lost, who had never returned.
Starting over was tough once again.
The war was over for everyone but them.
Give me a chance to forget where I've been,
But country and men
Would blame them for where they had been!

So quiet they became,
To not hear the shame.
So anger and hatred grew all the same.

How can I help, they never did hear.
Who would sit down to cry with them?
Your stories of woe let's not hear again.

Recover they try, hard as it is.
Give them a chance, to return once again.
To become what they can,
As they were once trying to do, before the war began!

Old Buddy of Mine

While in the military, servicemen meet many individuals they become close to, whom they call their buddies. One quickly learns how to make buddies. For those individuals that work closely, under stress (whether in the bush, on flights, river boats, submarines, Special Forces and others), there is a comradery that cannot be compared to anything that is enjoyed anywhere else. As buddies quickly enter one's life, they also leave one's life, whether it was due to death or the buddy being transferred or you being transferred. Because buddies enter and leave one's life so quickly, you get very close, but you don't allow yourself to let anyone get that close. You always keep your distance. This poem is dedicated to the buddies we came to have and love while we were in the military.

I often think of you, old buddy of mine.
That trusted companion you were of mine.
I think of the duty we shared, both you and me.
I think of the liberty we had together, both you and me.

How quickly we got to know each other.
The things we did share,
How we both missed home,
And how we would not lose touch, when we got back home.

How we did enjoy such close comradery.
We never had too much, or too little at that,
Because whatever we had we shared it together,
Closer we became, than brothers at home.

I remember the things we did,
The times we shared,
The jokes we played,
And the jokes we told.

I remember the places we went,
The beers we had,
And the stories we had,
About the liberty we had.

I remember the tears that were shed,
When our separate ways we did go.
I never forgot you, old buddy of mine,
But when you left, I tried not to remember too much.

Agent Orange

This poem is dedicated to all of those who have suffered from the effects of Agent Orange, a defoliate agent that was used in the Viet Nam War. The troops were never told how deadly it really was, and they were allowed to play with it. Many would use squirt guns to play with it. Many have lost their lives due to the effects of Agent Orange, and many are still suffering from the painful effects of it. The treatment they found to help was gold, which attract impurities in the body that Agent Orange introduced. The treatments are very painful, but without them those suffering will die sooner.

Lt. Col. James G. Zumwalt (son of Admiral Zumwalt and brother of Elmo Jr., who succumbed to the effects of Agent Orange) wrote wonderful book, titled "Bare Feet Iron Will Stories from the Other Side of Vietnam's Battlefields. On pages 6-8 he writes extensively about Agent Orange.

Agent Orange, orange in color it was,
Defoliating agent is what the troops were told it was.
The poison it really was,
The troops were never told that is what it was.

There was the D.M.Z., an imaginary line,
No troops could cross that imaginary line,
But Agent Orange had no boundary line,
Used on friendly and enemy troops, along that line.

The truth about Agent Orange,
From the Troops it was kept secret.
The Troops they played with it,
From squirt guns it came forth

The truth about Agent Orange,
For years it would not be told.
The government it would not tell,
The damage that was truly done.

The truth about Agent Orange,
The government would not admit,
Even though the Troops,
They would succumb to it!

The truth about Agent Orange,
The government would not tell it.
Even though children from Troops
Would be suffering from it.

Agent Orange, no boundaries did it know,
All who were under it, suffering they would come to know.
All who were under it, pain they would come to know.
All who were under it, dying they would come to know.

Price for Freedom

I never have to wonder what I would do, if the price for freedom I had to pay.
For the price of freedom I did have to pay.
I survived, only to be called a baby killer.
I survived, only to be called a mother raper.

I survived, but there was still a price to pay.
I survived, only to learn to draw blood, as my tongue I had to bite,
To ease the pain of being called many names,
By those who never had to pay the price for the freedom they have.

I survived, knowing I came so close to pay the ultimate price.
The price for freedom is no small price to pay.

Protestors

During the Viet Nam War there were many protesters. Where did they come from? What did they want? What were they for? What were they against? Many there were, at first they were small. Then as the war grew on, more and more there became. At first there was college deferment that kept them from the draft. Then that was not enough, married they had to be to keep the deferment. Then that was not enough, one child they had to have. Then that was not enough, more children they had to have. At first they burned draft cards, and then they burned flags. At first they protested the war, and then they protested the G.I.s.

At first there was a war,
In a land called Viet Nam.
Only advisors were the first to go,
Then the troops were sent after them.

When the advisors did go,
It was only a few hundred that did go.
Then as the war grew,
Hundreds after them did go.

When the troops did go,
It was only a few thousand that did go.
Then as the war grew,
Thousands more went after them.

Then as the war grew more and more,
Thousands upon thousands did follow them,
Until hundreds of thousands were in the foreign land.

As the war grew more and more,
More started to protest the war in Viet Nam.
At first there were thousands,
Then hundreds of thousands,
Finally more protesters than soldiers in Viet Nam.

Protesters at first were peaceable,
In protesting the war.
They felt it was wrong,
And men should not go to war.

Then as they grew,
More violent they became.
Their draft cards they did burn,
In protest of that war.

Then as they grew more and more,
Flags they began to burn, as more violent they became.

Then as the war grew, draft notices they got,
But stand up and fight they would not.
They chose rather to run in great fright.
Cowards they became and not in good light.

At first when there were few,
The government they protested.
Then as they grew more and more,
The G.I.s they protested even more.

As the protester grew,
The cry was heard throughout the land,
"Don't send anymore,
And bring the others out of that foreign land."

They held their rallies, saying "no more war."
Chanting "bring the troops home"
They had their signs about peace, love and more.
They said we should be doves, and hawks no more.

Then at their height,
As the G.I.s did come home,
They did not greet them
With peace and love that they had chanted at home.
No hugs did they give, to the G.I.s as they came home.

Then at their height, the G.I.s they did fight.
The G.I.s came home and they yelled at them with their might.
"Baby Killers and Mother Rapers"
They called those who came home.

They did not stop there, but grew in their shame.
They spit in their faces, and called them more names.
Some they did push, and others they did maim.
All this they did in ending the war good name.

As the G.I.'s returned from the war,
The protests did not end.
Now they protested the G.I.s returning,
Whom before they had wanted home.

Then when the war ended,
The protest should have also ended.
No more any war to blame,
So the G.I.s they blamed, for the war that had ended.

Where the protests to end the war,
Or what were they for?
If ending the war is what the protests were for,
Then ending the war should have made the protests no more!

In the end the protesters,
Were protesting for the sake of protesting.
Ending the war was not what they were for.
Protest for the sake of protesting is what they were after for.

If their protests where to end the war,
Then when the G.I.s returned after war,
They should have spent their time cheering,
Instead they spent their time jeering.

For the most part, for lack of good name,
Most the protesters became a big shame.
Some became politicians, to an even greater shame!

Post-Traumatic Stress Disorder

I don't feel well and I don't know why,
I don't feel well and the doctors can't find anything wrong
I don't feel well, but why, there doesn't seem to be anything wrong.

I can't be sick, I don't have a temperature.
I can't be sick, I don't have any pain.
I can't be sick, nothing is broken.

It has been this way for many years,
Why don't I get better, if there is nothing wrong?
Is it all in my head, like so many have said.

South bound on interstate 5,
Passing mile marker 124.

My heart pounds, louder and louder,
I am now alert, but what have I done?
Where am I and how long have I been out?

I don't recognize what I now see around me.
I now see the sign, mile marker 144
Oh my, what have I done, why has it happened once again?

Awake I am, but where have I been,
What was I thinking, I can't even recall.
I don't remember, as I begin to shake and gasp for air.

OOPS, how can that be,
How did I get here?
What was I thinking for the past twenty miles?

Don't Reject Me

Don't reject me because you and I are not quite alike.
Don't reject me because you think I'm different than you would like.

Don't reject me because I'm not what you heard I would be.
Don't reject me because I'm not what you thought I would be.

Don't reject me because of what I wanted to be.
Don't reject me because I'm not what you remember me to be.

Don't reject me because you did not serve.
Don't reject me because I served where you don't like.

Don't reject me because of where I've been.
Don't reject me because you've not been where I've been.

Don't reject me because I do what you can't.
Don't reject me because you do what I can't.

Don't reject me because I've done what you haven't.
Don't reject me because you've done what I haven't.

Don't reject me because I can't do what you do.
Don't reject me because I do what you don't do.

Don't reject me because I'm not where you would like me to be, at all.
Don't reject me because you don't understand me after all.

Don't reject me because I don't compare to the rest.
Don't reject me because I don't act like the rest.

Don't reject me because I don't say what you like.
Don't reject me because I don't act as you like.

Don't reject me because of my past, a past that you think you know so well.
Don't reject me because of my past, a past you do not know very well at all.

Don't reject me at all,
Because in the end you and I, are after all, much alike.
It you reject me, it's because you reject in me what you see in yourself!

River of Tears

River of tears, she just starts with something so slight.
River of tears, how she has poured forth with might,
River of tears, how she has burst forth and stayed all night,
When I wanted the river out of sight, she just burst forth with all her might.

River of tears, from where does she start?
River of tears, oh, where does she end?
River of tears, from what course does she follow?
River of tears, from what course does she stray?

River of tears, how long will you run?
River of tears, how fast will you flow?
River of tears, why can't a trickle you sometimes be?
River of tears, Oh, why must you always be so mighty and strong?

River of tears, oh, when will you cease?
River of tears, will you never dry up?

River of tears, will you ever become a stream,
And just one day, dry up and stop?

What Was Said Back Over Here

What did we hear when we came back from that war?
Many were the words that hurt to hear?
Words that vets heard when they came back from the war.

There are all crazy from fighting in that war.
They are now crazy from that war.
They are not normal, when they returned from that war.

Drugs they now take, to get relief from that war.
They do not know how to fit back in,
So, drugs they all take, because they can fit back in.

They are all violent, when they returned from the war.
They are so violent; they can't be trusted at all.
They are so violent; you're not safe when they are around.

They are so lazy, when they returned from the war.
They have forgotten how to work, back over here.
They will not last, in a job back over here.

Why can't they just get on with their lives?
When they get back over here?
Why can't they forget what happened over there?
Why do they remember what was so bad over there?

They just can't adjust to life back over here.
They can't keep a job, back over here.
That's why they steal and rob back over here.
That's why so many are in prison back over here.

All they seem to do when they get back over here,
Is complaining about what it is like after they came back over here.
They are nothing but crybabies and whiners, when they get back here.

What is wrong with them, when they get back here?
Why can't they pick-up where they were,
Before they went over there?
Why can't they learn that the war is now over, back over there?

Why can't they adjust and be like the rest of us?
Why are they different and not like the rest of us?
What is wrong with them, for not returning the same?

We would have been better,
If they had not returned back here.

Life was better, while they were gone over there.
It was much better, when they were away from here.

Scorned

Scorned by the world they were,
Scorned for being soldiers and sailors fighting in a war they were.
Scorned by their country, for fighting a war.

Scorned by their country, which asked them to fight that war.
Scorned by their nation, which protested that war.
Scorned by protesters, for fighting in that war,
Scorned by cowards, who ran from that war.

Scorned by family and friends,
When they returned back from that war.
Scorned by their nation,
Who raised up their arms and spit in their faces,
When they returned from that war!

Scorned they did feel, by a nation that was not real.
Alone they were made to feel,

They were not allowed to recover from that war,
    They were scorned for just being in war.

My Shell

An outer shell I have,
Hard as rock it is,
It cannot be penetrated.

For protection and defense, it was made.
To protect that soft, vulnerable person I am.
Few can pass through that hard-outer shell,
To find the real person that I am.

The hard-outer shell I built,
Is opposite from the real person I am.
The hard- outer shell feels no pain,
The real person inside is hurt so easily.

The hard-outer shell, rough it is,
The real person, so soft and gentle he is.
The hard-outer shell so abrasive and crude it can be,
The real person, so generous and gentle he is.

The hard-outer shell, emotionless it is.
The real person, so many tears it has shed.
The hard-outer shell, deceive you it will,
So, the person inside, can remain hidden and safe.

The hard-outer shell, so real it has become,
That I no longer know if I am real or the shell!

Since the Day

On this day of Memorial I am going to remember;
All the years I have had, since the day I should have died.
All the jokes I have told and heard, since the day I should have died.
All the jobs I have had, since the day I should have died.

All those that have wronged me, since the day I should have died.
All those that have helped me, since the day I should have died.
All those that have hugged me, since the day I should have died.
All those I have helped, since the day I should have died.
All those times, both good and bad, since the day I should have died.

Then I will ponder about what I would have missed, if I would have died.
Then I will give thanks for all I have endured, since the day I should have died.
It could have been better or worse, since the day I should have died.
But, at least I survived and didn't die,
So that I could enjoy my life, since the day I should have died.

Stairway

I am at the top of the stairway, which to me is somewhere I know.
But, the stairway below, for me, leads to nowhere I know.
At the top of the stairway I know where I am.
I am where the rain and sunshine does not dare to beat down.
I am somewhere I can curl up and call my home,
Even for just a moment in time.

But the stairway below, where it leads I am not sure I even want to know.
Why should I leave this place, because I am sure where I am.
But, down the stairway is where they want me to go.
They want me to be far away from where I am and where I know.

The stairway, for them, leads to somewhere they know!
The stairway, for me, leads to somewhere I do not know.
So many stairways, that I've been at the top,
Only to go down to where I surely know not.

Now once again I must leave the top of the stairway,
That leads down to somewhere I know not the way.
In hopes another I might sooner hope to find.
Where for a while it will be home and I hope no one will mind.

Standing On the Corner

As I stand on the corner, all alone and forlorn,
I watch the people pass-by, out of the corner of my eye.
I dare not look them directly in the eye,
For they are so much better than I.

If only one kind soul could find their hand to my cup.
Instead, heads turn and stern looks turn me to shame.

As I stand on the corner can anyone not see I am hurting inside?
Can anyone not see I have value as a human?
Can anyone not see I am not asking for a handout?
I am asking for help.

Can anyone not see I am not asking to shine?
I just want to be seen as someone who's fine.

No one deserves to be looked down upon.
No one deserves a disgusted look, because important they don't seem to be.

Your helping hand will not make me rich,
But it will help me to eat.

A Story to Tell

I have a story to tell,
But who will dare to listen to this story I tell?
It's a story of woe I do choose to tell,
But you did say, "It's not a story of woe we want you to tell."

My heart is reaching out, for this story of woe to tell.
Will you cry with me?
My mind is bringing out,
What happened so long ago?

You've never been there,
And say "how can that be,
I've never seen such a thing,
Such a story I have never heard before.

My mind digs deeper, do you stop me or do you let me go?
Will you let me bring it out, so I can admit it and go on?
Or do you stop me, so I can remember it some more?

The Zing and Thud I Can Never Forget

One day when all was so quiet,

All of a sudden all Hell did break loose,

When out of the dark there were flashes and bangs.

When to my surprise I heard these zings,

That by my head they did pass me by.

So close they did come, that they sounded like zing's.

Then all of a sudden one zing I did hear,

Followed by a "THUD", the likes I had not heard before.

It was a deafening sound, one awful sound to hear.

When all was again quite as before,

I turned to look at my buddy, who was behind,

He was not standing, but was flat on the ground and in red he was covered.

It was then that I fully realized,
That last zing I had heard, that was followed by that awful thud,
Was the zing my buddy had not heard and he had not heard the awful thud.

It was the thud I heard and the zing he never heard,
That thud that still echoes in my mind,
That thud I can never forget, no never forget.

To Care

To care for others,
Means considerate of others be.

To be considerate,
Means concerned of others be,
Concerned of them, and their feelings be.

To be concerned,
Means to speak to them, and not quite remain.

To speak to them,
Means to say what benefits them.

To benefit others,
Means to be uplifting to them.

To uplift others,
Means to better make them feel.
Better feel about life and themselves.

To make others feel better,
Means to not make them feel worse,
But means to think of them and not of self.

To think of others,
Means concerned of them be.

To be concerned of others,
Means to care for them well.

A True Friend

There are times, in everyone's life, when they need someone to share without any expectations in return. I once wrote a poem about such a person, "A True Friend." It was about my vision of what a true friend would be like. I never found such a person. If you ever find such a person enjoy their company while it lasts. I hope you find such a person.

A true friend is dear to the heart,
For with a true friend
Your heart can be opened up
And entirely exposed.

A true friend will listen
And let you bear your heart and soul.
A true friend with you
Will tears they shed
When your tears they begin to fall.

A true friend will joyful be
When you have joy to share.
A true friend will encouragement offer
A true friend will consoling be.

A true friend will also be open and honest
With feelings from the heart that come to mind.
A true friend will be there to offer help
With whatever is needed at that moment in time.

A true friend will be there
When others are not around.
A true friend will be there
When others have long gone by.

A true friend will help you
To be the best you can be.
A true friend is lasting
And always around
Never deserting when times they get tough.

True friends expect nothing
But receive what is best,
Another true friend at last at my side.

Death of a Viet Nam Vet

This poem is dedicated to all Viet Nam Vets that have died since the war. Those vets served their country and fought in a very unpopular war. Each and every one one of them deserves to be remembered.

When they were young, they accepted the call.
The call from the President to serve
And to fight in a war, in a faraway land.

Without thought of himself,
He did serve on behalf others,
Not saving his life, but to save the lives of others.

He gave up his rights,
To fight so others might be free,
And enjoy their rights.

He was from the land of the free and the brave,
Because of him it's what makes it the land of the brave,
Because of him it's what keeps it the land of the free.

In that war, in the faraway land,
He saw what had been done, in that far away land,
And he never forgot what he had done, in that far away land.

He was a very young man, when he went to that far away land,
In that far away land, he aged way beyond his years,
Because of the war that he fought in that land.

As he grew older he was deeply distressed,
By all that he saw and all that he did,
In the war in that far away land

For the rest of his life he was deeply pained,
By all those he saw that were greatly maimed,
And by all those who died and never remained,
Always to wonder why he was allowed to remain.

In that war a changed man he became
Never to be the same as he had once been before
Then only to be remembered by what he was after the war
And people always wondered why he wasn't like before!

The day he passed away, it was a sad day for all,
Because this country lost a once great fighting man,
Who in war for his country had given his all.

Arrangements now made, the final service takes place.
Words are now said for this man of great face,
And how in our hearts, he now dwells in a great place,
And for the rest of our lives, he will rest in that place.

We begin to remember all that he did,
And the great loss we now begin to sense
For the loss of this great fighting man,
Who once was a very fine stature of a man.

The Honor Guard now stands,
And takes the flag in their hands,
Now at attention they do stand,
Salute one another as the flag exchanges hands.

Tapps is now played for the final time,
Not to be heard by this very fine man,
But to be played in honor of this once fighting man,
This time it is played to tribute this great man.

With the flag in their hands,
It is now placed and given into the hands,
Of those who still love this great fighting man.

This once great fighting man, to rest he is now laid,
He is now at peace with the God who once had him made.
And finally he is free from all that he endured,
The suffering and pain will forever be gone.

That Viet Nam Buddy of Mine!

That Viet Nam buddy of mine,
Who I didn't even know had been sent to a foreign land,
And I never saw, when he was in Viet Nam.

How very proud I was,
When I heard that you served,
Those honors and medals you deserved.

I know it did hurt, for all that you saw.
I know it was painful, to see others you know fall.
I know it was sad, to think of home and all
I know it was miserable,
On the ground, in the mud, and under the rainfall.

I know how you wanted a hot meal to have,
Surrounded by friends and music to hear.

But all you did have, was a cold meal in a tin,
With bullets and mortars being the music you did hear.

How happy I was to know you survived.
How happy I was to hear you returned.
How happy I was to know you were alive.
How happy I was to know you made it back.

I wish I had been there the day you arrived,
I would have welcomed you back with a hug,
On that day you arrived.
I would have said to you then
"Welcome back and I'm glad you survived."

A hero's welcome you deserved,
You should have been cheered,
And with a big band been greeted
On the day that you returned.

In a parade you should have marched
And cheering crowds you should have heard as you passed by.
Waving flags you should have seen,
From the crowds you passed by

The day should have been yours,
Because the glory you deserved!
From the mayor you should have been greeted,
And a speech you should have heard.

At days end, in a line you should have stood,
For all to shake hands, and say you did good.
For all to say they were proud of you, as you stood.
For them to say, "Welcome back and were glad you made it back."

That's how you should have been greeted,
On the day you returned.
That's how you should have been treated,
On the day you returned.

The Wall

This poem is dedicated to all Viet Nam Vets whose names appear on the Vietnam Veterans Memorial Wall in Washington, D.C.

On this great Wall, are the names of them all,
Who in a war, gave it their all,
And now their names will be remembered, forever, after all!

Many a tear has been shed, at this great Wall.
Many a tear will be shed, at this great Wall.
So many tears that a great river could flow from that wall,
So many tears, that a mighty sea could be made from them all!

Many have made the journey back to the Wall,
All wondering why their buddies had to fall,
Why their buddies lives had to end, no longer to stand tall,
Why that fate, to them had to befall?

Many have made the journey back to the Wall,
Wondering why they were allowed to return,
While their buddies had to fall?
What made them so special that they did not fall?

Many have made the journey back to the Wall,
Wondering why their names did not appear on the Wall,
Wondering why they themselves did not fall,
Why they themselves did not have to die after all?

Many have made the journey back to the Wall,
Wondering how close they came to having their name on the Wall?
Wondering if they would be remembered, or be just another name on a Wall?
Wondering, if they would have been missed at all?

Many have not made the journey back to the Wall,
Always wondering if they went to the Wall,
Would they see their names on it after all?

War

If you should decide,
Another war to fight,
Make sure it is fought
In a way that is fought to win

If you should decide,
To send men again,
Make sure they are sent,
To a war they are to win.

Do not let them go,
And in vain be slain.
Let them die with honor,
In fighting a war to win.

When they return,
Proud of them be.

Show them the honor,
They deserve to have showered on them.

Let them accept their place
And be proud they have returned.
Let them return,
And in honor be received.

War at Its Best

War at its best, is the worst life can get.
War at its best, should never be seen by any at all.
War at its best, will forever be with those that have seen it.

War at its best, only bad memories does it bring forth.
War at its best, only bad feelings does it arouse.
War at its best, brings the worst of thoughts right to the fore.

War at its best, makes men the worst they can be.
War at its best, makes men as bad as they can possibly be.
War at its best, makes men hated by those they don't even know.

War at its best, changes men for the rest of their lives.
When war we have seen and seen it at its best,
Then we know we have seen life the worst it can be!

I've Been Watching

Many youths watch their parents suffer through the after effects of war. The parent feels that the child cannot understand what they have been through and therefore never talks to the child about the suffering they go through. The child on the other hand sees the parent cry. The child sees the parent get angry and may even see the parent get abusive. The child may not understand the war, but they certainly do thoroughly understand the after effects of war.

I never knew what you were like before, before you went away.
Before I was born, when you were far away,
Fighting in a land I never hear you mention, that is so far away.

You think I can't understand the pain that you have inside,
You think I can't understand the hurt you have carried inside,
You think I can't understand the hatred you feel inside.

You may be right, I might not be able to understand it at all, today.
But, I do understand the pain I see you are in today,
I can only understand what I see, and I see a lot today.

If you don't tell me about what I see in you today
How can I ever understand what you feel inside today?
How can I ever understand what I see day after day?

I see the tears in your eyes, and you say they are not tears at all.
I hear your screams, while you are asleep, in the hall.
And all you say is "it was nothing at all."

I see you shake and sweat, for no reason at all, inside this house we're in.
And all you can say is that "it is cold inside this house", the house we're in
But, outside it is a hot summer day,
And I am sweating because of the heat in this house we're in.

I see you duck, when a loud bang we hear.
And all you say is "what was that I hear?"
And then you say, "I don't understand why I ducked at all,
I just thought it was near."

I hear you scream at me, for no reason at all.
Later you say you are sorry for screaming at me for no reason at all
But, you never say why you screamed at me at all.

I see movies about people like you and how they are.
Why do I have to learn from the movies about why you are the way you are?

Why can't I learn that from you?
Because I know I'll learn better from you why you are the way you are.

No, I don't understand why you are the way you are.
But, if you talked to me and told me why you are the way you are
Then I just might understand and not become like you are!

This is what I have learned from you, because of the way you are.
I cannot talk about what hurts me inside, because of the way you are.
I must keep it a secret, because we don't talk about the way we are.

I want to share with you, the way I feel inside.
But, I have not been taught how to share what is inside.
I have not been taught how to talk about what is inside.

You are right when you say I cannot understand,
Because, you have not helped me to understand,
What you don't know is that you kept from me
That which you think I can't understand.

I just might be able to understand if you talked to me,
About what I don't understand.
If you talked about what it is that you don't think I can understand
I possibly might learn how to understand what you think I can't understand.

You think riddles is what I speak, because you don't understand,
It is riddles you speak about what you think I can't understand.
If we both talked about what we don't understand,
Then maybe we would understand.

And then instead of riddles to speak,
We would have love we could understand.

I have learned from you to keep things all bottled up inside.
I have learned from you to not talk about what hurts me inside.
I have learned from you not to let others get close,
So that they don't know what I am on the inside.
I have learned from you to say, "nothing is wrong,"
When everything is wrong on the inside.

Someday I hope I can find someone that will talk
So I can then learn from them how to talk back in return
So that I can reveal what causes my pain.

When someday I find someone that will talk,
Then someday I will learn to you how to better talk,
And let you know,
I really do understand and it's something about which we really can talk.

Your pain I also feel, because I see the way you are and not the way you were.
I really do understand, because of what I see in you.
I really do understand, because of how I was treated by you.

What I Thought Would Happen

I served my country well, or at least I thought it was well.
I fought in a war, which was in a faraway land,
And came close to death, but continued to fight with honor.

Medals I received, for actions I was engaged in.
Commendations mounted, the longer I served and the longer I stayed in.
Then my time came, and bound for my land I was.

I was scarred from where I had been,
But I was proud I had served and I was coming back.
I did not know what would happen when I returned,
But I thought I would see all, when I got back.
I had ideas of what I thought would happen, when I came back.

When I got back, I thought I would be greeted and maybe even treated.
I thought I would be met with happy faces

From those I thought would be glad I survived.
I thought there would be some with an outstretched hand to greet me.

Others I thought might give me a hug
And say to me, "We are happy you are back alive."
I even thought some would pat me on the back
And say I am glad you did that.

Others I thought would say they were proud that I had done what I did.
I thought memories of old would be rekindled, by those I once knew.
And former friendships would pick up like they once had been before.

I thought it was with respect and understanding I would be treated.
I thought there would be those that cared enough
And by them I would be greeted.
I thought there would be those that would ask how I had been.

I knew it would not be easy,
But the worst I thought was gone and behind me.
I was wrong about what I thought would happen.
Because, what I thought would happen never happened at all!

When I Came Back

Where were you when I came back?
Where were you, old friend of mine?
When you needed me then, I was at your side,
But now that I am in need, no one's at my side!

Where were you when I came back?
Where were you, when I needed a hug?
Where were you, when a story I needed to tell?
Where were you, when the tears they came forth?

Where were you when I came back?
Old friend of mine, where were you when I came back.
I never forgot you, old friend of mine.
I never forgot you, old friend of mine.

Where We Go

I would like to think there is a place where we all go.
A place where pain, suffering and sorrow are no more.
A place where we all go and we are free after all.
Free to be what we always wanted to be.

A place where we can go and can't remember the pain at all.
A place where can go and there are no limits at all,
No limits to stop our progress from being the best after all.

Where everyone is just neighbors to one and all,
Where everyone helps because it's the right thing to do.
Where no one has too much at all and no one else lacks anything at all.

I would like to think there is a place we all go
Where we learn our old life was only temporary,
And this new place is a permanent one and it is for all.

A place where we learn the truth about everything
And it costs nothing to anyone at all
And it's the truth that is the same for all.

A place where the pain and suffering we saw,
Will never again be that way for anyone at all.
A place where never again will tears ever flow.

A place where the rivers are clean
From the streams to the oceans as they flow.
Where the air we breathe is fresh from morning dawn to dusk at night.

A place where all neighborhoods are the best they can be.
A place where no one will bring harm to his fellow man,
Who are all brothers and sisters to everyone that is there.

This is the place I would like to think we all go.
This is the place we should all like to go.
This is the place I would like to think is where we all live forever more.

Who Am I?

For over twenty years, after being discharged from the military, I was called Chuck; I would not allow anyone to call me Charlie (the name I had been called before I was drafted). This is something that I have found out that many have done, not being called by the name they were known before they went into the military.

This poem is dedicated to the man that helped me break the final barrier, which allowed me to finally start becoming myself.

Off to war Charlie went,
Many friends saying, "We'll miss you over there."
Companions a many, saying, "Hurry home and we'll party over here."
Friends, how good they were, in words and intents.
But while Charlie was gone, the friends left too!

Off to war Charlie went,
Dreams shattered and hopes crushed.

A new life he had to take,
A new identity he would have.

Soon Charlie was dead and Chuck was alive.
Poor Chuck, friends he had none,
No one cared for Chuck, gone astray.

Then a former friend we did met.
As we talked he wondered, "What has Charlie become?"
I do not know this man I once knew so well,
He is now a complete stranger to me and this stranger I don't like!

He wondered about Charlie, "What have you become?"
I became what I became, for protection you know.
You wondered why did I become what I became?
I became what I did because of life.
You wondered how did I become what I did.

My only answer, I became what I did because,
Because life pulled this way and that way,
Because life put up blocks, ones that you have not seen!
I had to go under, around, over or through
Because life opened some doors,
But mostly because life closed many doors.

As you parted your thoughts ran deep.
Old friend, I know you not,
But Charlie I knew well.
Old friend, you're not like the Charlie I knew so well.

You're not friendly and fun, you're not full of spirit and life,
Like Charlie I loved and once knew so well

Then Chuck returned, with Charlie still dead and gone.
Old Charlie would try to jump out,
But, Chuck would say, "No," and protect him again.

Chuck is so strong, Charlie so vulnerable.
Will Charlie ever come out, or will Chuck keep him in?
Charlie wants out, so he can live once again.
Who will help Charlie to live once again?

Charlie was hid so well,
Hid so well even Chuck forgot who Charlie once was.
Will Charlie ever return to life,
And live once again?

The barrier so great,
It cannot be broken by itself.
Try as he might, Charlie is trapped.
How will he get out, to be free again.

Then the Old Friend does call once again,
To Chuck he talks about the Charlie he once knew.
Charlie inspired me so well,
Yes, I remember that, now that you recall.
Charlie was tough, and fight he did well.
Yes, I remember that, now that you recall.

As we talk, Old Friend and I,
Charlie is coming to life once after all.
As we do talk, Chuck begins to die,
And Charlie is starting to live once after all.

The more you recall,
The more Charlie is coming to life.
Yes, I now remember so well,
Yes, I am the Charlie you knew well.
Yes, I am now Charlie, alive and well.

Old Friend, you brought Charlie to life, once and for all.
Old Friend, you eased the pain, and brought Charlie to life.
Old Friend, thank you for looking,
Thank you for searching, thank you for finding,
And thank you for healing,
Thank you for bringing Charlie back to life!

Why Am I Here?

Why am I here in this far away land? I am told it's our enemies land.

But, this is not like the training I received for fighting in this far away land.

Who is the enemy, I am supposed to fight in this far away Land?

How do I tell the difference between our friend and our foe?

When they all look alike, both our friend and our foe!

They all dress alike and there are no signs that say

This is my friend or this is my foe.

How different they are in this land, from what I was taught back in my home-land.

Not all are so bad, like what I was taught, back in my homeland.

Many are kind and treat me with respect,

And not mean like I was taught back in my homeland.

The fighting is far worse, when I'm actually involved.

I see the worst that war can involve.

The bad is far worse, than what I was taught it would involve.

What makes it worse, is it's not always that bad.
But, when it is bad, it's worse than I thought it could possibly be.
I was not trained for what I do see;
I was trained for what others thought it would be.

All I do know, is I don't like what I see, and I don't like where I have to be.
I see the worse, that mankind can possibly be.
At times, I see the worst in myself, far worse than I thought I could ever be.

I never thought they were as bad as they are.
I never thought I could be as bad as I am.
I never thought I could do what I have done.

Why am I here, in this far away land?
How do I fight the enemy, in this far away land?
They are not the same in the day and the night;
There is a big difference between day and night.

During the day, they are as kind as can be.
But, during the night, they are worse they can be.
How can they change, from day through the night, and so different be.

All I do know is the orders they surely do flow.
What I am told, I must follow it through.
What I am told, I must not question at all.

What I have learned, is that I must do as I am told, or I will surely die.

And it's not mine to reason why, mine is just to do or die!

And if I do as I'm told, there's still a chance I might still die!

Why Me?

So many young men and good ones at that,
Lost their lives and never came back.
Why me, why did I survive and make it back?

Some were much stronger than I,
But, their strength couldn't save them in the end.
Yet, I, who was not as strong was saved, why me?

Some were much smarter than I,
But, their smarts did not save them in the end.
Yet I, who was not as smart made it through the end, why me?

Some were more talented than I,
However, their talent did not protect them in the end.
Yet I, who was not as talented survived the war, why me?

Some were much kinder than I,
But, in the end their kindness did not help them get through.
I on the other hand, who was not as kind, did get through, why me?

Some were very lucky at all they did,
But, their luck ran out and they did not last.
Yet my luck did not run out, why me?

Some were from families that loved them so much,
Yet their family's love did not help them at all.
But my family such love they did not show and I lived, why me?

Some were far more religious than I.
But, in the end their beliefs and religious ties were no protection at all.
I was not religious at all and lived, why me?

Why me, why did I survive
When so many others, who were much better than I,
Did not survive?

Those many good men died and a short lifetime they lived.
I who was not as good have a much longer life that I have lived.
Why should I have lived and much better men than I not have lived?

I guess the reason I survived was because
I was not at the wrong place at the wrong time
And my surviving had nothing to do with anything at all.

So many young men and good ones at that,
Lost their lives and never came back.
Why me, why did I survive and make it back?

Some were much stronger than I,
But, their strength couldn't save them in the end.
Yet, I, who was not as strong was saved, why me?

Some were much smarter than I,
But, their smarts did not save them in the end.
Yet I, who was not as smart made it through the end, why me?

Some were more talented than I,
However, their talent did not protect them in the end.
Yet I, who was not as talented survived the war, why me?

Some were much kinder than I,
But, in the end their kindness did not help them get through.
I on the other hand, who was not as kind, did get through, why me?

Some were very lucky at all they did,
But, their luck ran out and they did not last.
Yet my luck did not run out, why me?

Some were from families that loved them so much,
Yet their family's love did not help them at all.
But my family such love they did not show and I lived, why me?

Some were far more religious than I.
But, in the end their beliefs and religious ties were no protection at all.
I was not religious at all and lived, why me?

Why me, why did I survive
When so many others, who were much better than I,
Did not survive?

Those many good men died and a short lifetime they lived.
I who was not as good have a much longer life that I have lived.
Why should I have lived and much better men than I not have lived?

I guess the reason I survived was because
I was not at the wrong place at the wrong time
And my surviving had nothing to do with anything at all.

The Best of Times and the Worst of Times

The worst is the death and destruction that is all around,
The best is when recovery will take place.
The best is the resting, and the worst is the fighting.

The best is a letter from home
And the worst is what's inside that letter from home.
The best is thinking about home
And the worst is thinking I might not go home.
The best is sleeping when I can
And the worst is waiting while I'm wide-awake.

The best is the rest and relaxation I've been given,
The worst is knowing I'll have to go back.
The best is a smoke my buddy gave me;
The worst is the smoke I gave my buddy on the ground.
The best is a hot meal ate at a table;
the worst is a cold meal right out of a can.

The best is a shower to clean off the grime;
The worst is to crawl in the mud and the slime.
The best is good music to hear,
The worst are the loud noises that ring throughout the night.
The best is knowing what lays ahead;
The worst is not knowing what actually lays ahead.

The best are hugs from those nearby;
The worst are no kisses from those far away.
The best are buddy's I've known a short time,
The worst are old friends who don't care I'm still alive.
The best are the times for thinking of the past,
The worst is thinking of the future that's ahead.

The best is the card game for killing time;
The worst is the time for killing those around.
The best is knowing there's an end to it all,
The worst is knowing I might not live to the end of it all.
The best is knowing some good I have done;
The worst is knowing that some bad I have done.

The best is knowing I did not run,
The worst is knowing I could have run.
The best are the jokes and the kidding around;
The worst is seeing what's actually all around.
The best is a quiet and bright moonlight;
The worst is a fiery skylight.

The best I'm told is what lays ahead,
The worst I am told is what I've just come through.
The best is seeing replacements come in,
The worst is knowing that some won't come out.
The best is the good news from back home,
The worst are the riots that I hear are back home.

The best was finally going back home
And the worst was finally going back home!

The Zing

There is a sound that cannot be understood,
Unless a person themselves has heard the sound.
That sound, as best it can be described, is "Zing."

"Zing" can only be heard if it passes by close
And the closer it comes, the louder it is.
The closer it passes the more distinct and clear its sound.

It is a sound that will never be forgotten.
Once it is heard, it is forever imbedded in one's mind,
And there it will stay and rear its ugly head when most unwanted.

Once the "Zing" has been heard, it can never be forgotten.
If it passes near enough, it is a sound that will echo
In your mind for many days to come.

The close it comes, the sharper its sound.
If it passes by close enough,
Then the wind, it can be felt.

When the "Zing" is heard and the wind is felt
One knows that is as close as it can get, and still be alive.
For if it passed any closer, no "Zing" would be heard.

For if it passes close enough, no "Zing" will you hear.
It is those nearby, that a "Thud" is what they will hear.

A thud is what is heard, by those nearby,
A thud, such a small hole it makes, when it goes in,
But, when it leaves, a much larger hole is what is left.

"Zing's" are frightening to hear, when you hear it yourself,
But, better for one, that a "Zing" he does hear,
Rather than his buddies nearby, a "Thud" they do hear.

Five from Foster Hi That Gave Their All

Foster High School (Seattle, Washington) has seen many graduate, who went on to become teachers, lawyers, legislators, doctors, dentists, engineers, nurses, and executives. Foster rightfully should be proud of them all. There is a special group of graduates that Foster High School should be notably proud of. That special group are all those who served in the military during the Viet Nam War and all other wars. It is not known exactly how many served, but it is known that scores of Foster Graduates did serve during the Viet Nam War. Some served as Marines, Soldiers, Sailors, and Air Force. Some that served left their blood in that foreign land, called Viet Nam, they were wounded in action. Then there are the special group of five, that gave the highest sacrifice that could be given. Foster High School should be especially proud of the five that gave their lives. This poem is dedicated to all those who served in that war, but, particularly to the five that gave their lives. This poem is dedicated to the memory of the Foster High School graduates who gave their lives and were killed in action in the Viet Nam War. There were five who died in that war and they are:

Clarence Sweeney (Class of 1951),
Arnold Nakkerud (Class of 1963),
Lawrence "Larry" A. Letterman (Class of 1964),
William (Buddy) Leander Erikson, Jr. (Class of 1966), and
Ed Howk (Class of 1967).

From the halls of Foster Hi,
Are those who in esteem are held high.
For doctors, lawyers and teachers they became
But others went on, to be remembered they became.

There was a war in Viet Nam,
Many did run, and cowards they were
To save their lives, the draft they did avoid.
But those from Foster Hi their duty they did not avoid.

Those that did run, shameful were they.
Those from Foster Hi, not shameful but proud were they.
Those from Foster Hi, not cowards were they.
Those from Foster Hi, indeed brave were they.

Class officers some were,
Football, basketball and baseball players others were.
Fine athletes and scholars they once were
Brave fighting men in war they were!

While Foster Hi they attended, champions once were they.
But more than champions became they,
One and all alike, heroes became they,
While in the military, heroes became they.

Those from Foster Hi, came from a fine breed,
Cowards they were not, but brave they were indeed.
Run they did not, but fight they did indeed,
And they should be remembered for that great deed.

They traded their freedom, and their rights they gave up.
They traded their freedom, to be ordered around.
They traded their freedom, to be told where to go.
They traded their freedom, so others freedom could enjoy.

From Foster Hi, there were those that served.
Some were drafted, the rest they enlisted and served.
In the Army, Navy, Marines and Air Force they served.
All took their chances, when in the Armed Forces they served.

All were standing straight and tall, when they left.
All could see and run with their might, when they left.
The power of youth they all possessed, when they left.
It was a different world for them, when they left.

When they returned they were not the same,
As boys they left, but as men they returned.
They saw in war, the worst that could be seen.
They saw in war, what the rest could not even dream.

In that foreign land called Viet Nam, they sacrificed.
With their blood, some sacrificed.
With their sight, some sacrificed.
With their limbs, others sacrificed.

All that served, knew that their life they could loose,
But follow their orders, they did to their best,
Orders they knew, that could cost them their lives.
Orders they knew, that would cost some lives.

Some came back with stars,
Bronze Stars and Silver Stars.
Some came back with Purple Hearts and battles scars,
All came back with inside scars.

Some came back with buddies they had made,
Others came back with only memories of buddies they had made.
Some came back with buddies who had to be buried,
Others came back to find buddies already buried.

All that served gave up something,
But some gave up more than all others.
Some gave up all, and gave up their lives,
In that foreign land, Called Viet Nam.

From Foster Hi, there were five that gave of their lives.
Let us never forget the five, that gave up their lives.

Let us never forget the five, that served above all others.
Let us never forget the five, that gave up their lives.

How proud we should be, of the five that lost their lives,
How happy we should be, that only five lost their lives.
Always remember the five that lost their lives,
And pray that no others will ever loose their lives.

The sacrifice was great, for family and friends,
For the family and friends, of the five that lost their lives.
They can never have back, the five that lost their lives.
Always remember the five that lost their lives!

Also remember the rest, who from Foster Hi they did come,
And remember they could have also lost their lives.
Never should we forget, any of those that served,
And could have lost their lives!

But, especially remember, the five that served,
And gave of their lives.
Always remember the five that served,
And gave up their lives.

Be proud of all those that served, who could have lost their lives.
Be the proudest of those that who served, and it did cost them their lives!
Honor all those that served, who could have lost their lives.
Honor those most that served, and it did cost them their lives!

Returning Vet's Saga

This is the poem that got it all started.

The following poem was written by me, a Viet Nam Veteran, who served in the United States Navy from 1969 through 1975, primarily on submarines. This is the story of my returning as a Viet Nam Veteran and the experiences I shared in common with many returning Viet Nam Veteran's. Upon arriving home all Viet Nam Vet's and Vietnam Era Vets were grouped together in one group and treated the same. It took fifteen years to put into words what I had felt after returning from the military, then few additional years to complete this work. As I wrote this poem many tears ran down my face. Each veteran that has received this poem has not been able to read it without shedding a tear or two. As some later told me, "The flood gates of the heavens opened up." The usual comment they make after reading this is, "I thought I was the only one that felt that way." The highest compliment that was given to me, for this poem, was from the girlfriend of one Vet. She obtained a copy of this poem to give to her boyfriend. When the two of them broke up and the Vet left her, he kept the copy of this poem for himself. Another extremely high compliment that was given to me was the following comment that was made to me: "All these years this is the way I felt, but I could not put it into words." Most veteran's that read the following poem ask me if they can keep it and naturally I say, "Yes." When those who are not veterans read the poem, they usually hand it back and say, "It was good." If you read this and do not fully understand, don't feel bad because only those that have served can understand what this poem really means.

Those that did not serve cannot thoroughly understand the feelings of those that did serve. Most that served were drafted and their lives were forever changed. In ten to twelve weeks they were changed from the person they once were, to a killing machine. They did not return the same person as they left. They were never re-trained to not be a killing machine, that they were expected to do all on their own. After they returned there were the sleepless nights, the light sleeping that went on for ten, fifteen, or more years, being awakened with the slightest noise or the slightest touch. Most all suffered, and may continue to suffer periods of depression (though others may not realize it). In an instant, they many may be back (flash back) to where they were serving: by a noise, by a smell, by a word or even by an action. Even today, the tears still come to their eyes, not as often, not as long as they first did, but they still come back once and a while. When many were discharged they were told, "don't tell anyone where you have been or what you have done. If you do we will come after you and you will be tried in a military court, not a civilian court."

Many often think about what they would have become if they had not served. All of those that went gave up something, gave up something that they were never given back when they returned. None, no matter where they served, came back the same as when they had left.

For those of you that are veteran's that read this, I want to extend to each and every one of you a warm welcome back home. "I am glad you survived and came back." Those words "I am glad you survived and came back, welcome back home" took me almost twenty years to hear, and it was from someone I didn't even know, nor have never seen. That individual asked me if I was a Viet Nam Vet and I responded by saying yes, while thinking in the back of my mind, "Oh, well, here it comes again!" Then they said those words "I am glad you survived and came back." It hit me, like a baseball bat between the eyes. I had never heard those words and I broke down and cried on the spot. It took me several minutes to regain my composure, then they started to apologize for bring back some bad memories. Then I explained to them why, concluding by saying that unkindness I have come to accept, but kindness is received so seldom (concerning my being a vet) that I just didn't know how to respond. So, to all you vet's that have returned, "I am glad you survived and glad you came back home, welcome home vets!"

I am also very proud of you for serving this country. Most of you did not ask to serve, but when this country asked you to serve you did not hesitate. You served and for this I am very proud of you. This poem is in honor of all that served and returned, and in honor of those that served and never returned. All you veterans that returned are heroes. You are heroes because you were not afraid to put your lives on the line, something that most living in this country today have never done. You put up with much while you were in, and you have put up with even more since you returned. You Veterans truly are the great American Heroes!

On top of the world, I was and a once kind, gentle person was I.
Goals I had and dreams I had, of better things ahead.
No cares did I have and no problems were around,
I was enjoying a life of delight,
With destiny under my control, and me controlling my destiny.
Life was good and it was great to be alive.

Then, one day, a letter I received,
From the President of the U.S. of A. it was sent.
I did not want to go, you know.
In fact I once said, "I would never go!"
But what would I do, what could I do?
I could not say, "Hell, no, I won't go!"
as many my age had already made known.

Torn away from the life I had and the life I was building, all on my own.
I went as I was asked, to serve for God, country and apple pie back home.
My President and government had asked me to go and I could not say, "No."
It was to protect my family, friends and to defend my country, that I called
home.
I was informed I would be fighting against a woeful aggressor,
So his deeds would not come to haunt my home!

So I departed and went where I was ordered to go.
Lifelong goals and dreams now shattered they had become.
New ones I would be granted, but simple they would now become.
Exactly what would I be, where would I go, what would I do?
How long would I live and would I ever return?
Questions I had and no answers were there to be found,
I would have to wait to see what the future was for me!

Off to war I went, like so many before and after me.
Leaving family, friends, wives and lovers, far behind me.
Young and innocent I was, returning I hoped, but dying I might.
Forgotten I became, unwanted I thought.

Off I went, young and innocent and hardened I became.
That kind, soft, gentle person that once was I,
Now became hard and abrasive and disillusioned was I.
A shell I built up, hard as a rock it became,
For protection and sanity it was made.

Before, life and dreams had surrounded me,
Now death, hurt and sorrow are all around me.
If I sleep would I live wake? If I woke would I live to sleep?
Alone and helpless I felt, with destiny now dominating and controlling me!

Fear, it became my constant companion and was always with me.
Will relief ever come to me?
Loneliness, so close we became.
Death, I stared it eye to eye, on many occasions I thought I would say bye!

Only I know how close I really came,
To this day I wonder why I survived, and others did not!
And now I wonder what significance my survival has really meant?

While serving in those foreign waters, a saying was heard over and over:
"Mine was not to reason why, mine was just to do or die!"

While serving family, friends, God and country, in that war torn land,
Letters I desired, but few I received.
Then one day a letter I received and it was written to me,
"Dear John, another I have found."
And I thought, "Oh, if only I had stayed that wouldn't have happened to
me?"
And I wondered, "Does no one longer care to stick by my side?"

New friends I now gained and buddies we were called
And mostly nicknames we had,
Moose, Tiny, Slim, Shorty, Sweet-Pea, Ski, Chicago,
Oly, Texas, Buzzard, Doc and much more.
But how close can I get to someone who is here today, but tomorrow is gone.
How much loss can my mind endure?
How much sorrow can my heart now endure?

Up and awake for a day, two, three or more, without sleep I went,
I had to stay awake and alert, because others depended on me.
And then came their turn, awake and alert they had to be,
And now I depended on them.

At times the intenseness was great,
No noise dared I make and no sound could I utter.
Quite and still I had to remain, all to stay undetected and hidden from those
who were around.
This I had to do so another day I could return for more of the same!

A country that loved me I once departed, to countries that hated me I arrived.
Un-liked I was, but never mistreated was I over there.
Then that day arrived, to return to a country that abhorred me back here.
Un-liked, unwanted and mistreated I now became over here.

Returned, I did and then left alone to recover from the death,
Hurt, grief and sorrow.
My stories of woe, you did not want to hear.
When I returned, where was the handshake, to welcome me back?
Where was the thank-you for the job I had done?
Where was the encouragement to move on ahead?
Where was the hug, to make me feel loved?

Where were the words "you're okay and everything will be fine?
Where were my friends, so many I once had?
Where was the thank-you, I needed to hear?
Where were the words, the kind words that would do so much good?
Where was the love I so desperately needed?

Where was the job I now needed, even more than before?
Why was there no one that to me could say, "I am proud of you for serving?"
And why did no one dare say, "I am glad you survived!"
And why did no one care to say, "I am glad you came back!"

And why was no one so kind to say,
"Welcome back home and were glad you're back alive!"

Hard it became, because work there was none.
"Hire a vet" was the saying heard loud and clear, throughout all the land.
But, country and men, wanted those that had stayed,
But not those who had served in that war torn land!

It caused me to wonder, "Where would I be, if only I had stayed?"
It made me think, "Where would I be, if served I had not?"
And then I began to ponder, "Who would I be, if only I had stayed?"
And the ringing in my mind became, "What would I be, if served I had not?"

On returning back here, it was angry faces and voices that I found in front of
me,
"Baby killer, mother raper" words they scolded and screamed at me,
But such things I had never considered, because that really wasn't me.
I only did as I was asked, so why are you scolding me?
Why all the anger that was directed at me?
Didn't they know that if they would have went, they would be just like me?
Didn't they know "I defended them, so they didn't have to go?"

The war was over for everyone,
But those that had went and had fought where they had been.
Give me a chance to forget where I've been.
But country and men would blame us for where we had been.
They blamed us for the problems they were in.

Where was the home I left so long ago?
This is not the same as I remember from before.
This was not the home I remember leaving, when I went off to war.
Away from home I was taken,
And never allowed to return to the home I once knew.
I returned, but it was not to the gentle life I had known before,
Rather, I returned to be scorned and hated, by those I had defended.

Then there were the cold sweats and nightmares, almost nightly for many a
year
How do I explain what's happening to me, how do I forget what happened to
me?
The tears, will they ever stop and they start for no reason at all?
Will anyone ever bother to gently wipe a tear from my eye?
Why is it so easy for them to bring tears to my eyes and they don't even notice?

Oh, if someone would just listen, oh, if someone would try to understand
The hurt I feel, the losses I have endured.
If I talk, who will dare to listen?
If you hear my story of woe, will you kindly listen?
Or will you say, "We've heard that story before?"
And will you add, "You cry babies are all the same,
You need to forget and get on with your life."

Now, I need help.
Where is my government, when I need them most of all?
I helped them when they needed it!
Who will defend me now, those I once defended?

The medals I wore over my heart while serving,
Have now become a burden my heart is bearing!

The frustration of war was bad,
The frustration of after war is overwhelming!
Will I ever be taken off of the battlefield?

In an instant, immediately I am back to where the danger was!
Reliving those life-threatening situations I once endured.
Again, so close to death I am,
Why am I here? What am I doing? Who cares about me?
No time to think, I must react.
Then the tears come,
And finally I once again return to the present.

That war torn, hardened shell, born for protection over there,
Now becomes harder and more battle scared back here
Because of the war I now fight back over here.

On occasion, I now drift to the place in my mind,
Where solitude and peace are all around!
A place I have made, of what I would like it to be.
A place to retreat when I need comfort and rest!
Only to regretful return to this place, I am now in.

Will I ever recover, fully recover?
Will my hard outer shell ever soften?
To let that kind, gentle person out,
That is hidden so well?

Will I ever again control my destiny?
Will I ever enjoy that life of bliss I once knew?
Will I ever recover, fully recover?

Will you remember me for what I once was?
Or will you remember what I have become?
Will you remember me for what I want to be?
Or will you remember what I have become?
Will you remember me for what I could have become?
Or will you remember what I have become?
Will you remember me for what I wanted to become?
Or will you remember me for what I really became?

Note: This poem was the most popular with veterans. The best compliment I was paid was when a vet's girlfriend took a copy home for her vet. I talked with the vet later and he told me, "My girlfriend left, but I kept the poem."

Appendix I: First Hand Accounts

Before I start with some actual experiences of Viet Nam Vet's I would like to mention a little about the draft. In the 60's and early 70's all eighteen year olds had to sign up for the draft. At first, few were drafted, but the number of those drafted kept increasing by the tens of thousands each year, until the Viet Nam War ended in 1973 and we finally pulled out in May of 1975. As the war continued to grow, year after year, some individuals did many things to avoid being drafted. At first a college deferment kept one out of the draft, some even became perpetual students. In the later years even a college deferment didn't keep ones out of the draft. Then if they were married it kept them out of the draft. Then as the war progressed they had to have at least one child, to be kept out of the draft. Then as the war grew, more and more, they had to have two children, or more, to be kept out of the draft. Some entered the National Guard and Reserves. None of the above were draft dodgers. It is true, they did avoid the draft, but they were not draft dodges. Draft dodgers were those, who after receiving their draft notices, failed to show up at the Induction Centers or even left the United States to avoid being drafted. This latter group were "Draft Dodgers." However, there were millions upon millions that did not try to avoid the draft. When they received their draft notices they accepted their responsibility and entered the military. The following are experiences of those who accepted that challenge and what they went through because of that acceptance and what they are still going through!

The following are actual experiences compiled from my own and those of other Viet Nam Veterans, or as some choose to say "Viet Nam Era Veterans." Only first names are used and sometimes I use fictitious first names, this is to protect the true identity of those who have told me their stories. The first few are my personal experiences and I include them because I have found out they are typical and not unusual for Viet Nam Vets to go through!

***

Dan

Dan was an Army Ranger, stationed in Viet Nam during the final days of that war. His assignment was to protect the Landing Zone (L.Z.) around the helicopter, while others went in to remove (take out) communist sympathizers, either to take them to safety or to terminate them. Most of the time all he heard was gunfire, very few were others taken out other than the Army Team. He was trained to detect any movement and shoot first and ask questions later. He was trained to act immediately. After his last mission, he returned to home base to be sent back to the United States for discharge. Three days after his last mission he was "walking the streets of the United States." His debriefing from the Army was as follows: "Don't tell anyone exactly where you were and what you did, or we will come after you and you will be tried in a military court not a civilian court!" This, by the way, was what most G.I.'s were told at their debriefing before being discharged! He was given no retraining, his natural instinct to kill (that had been developed by the Army) he would have to cope with and readjust on his own- which, by the way he did a marvelous job of doing. He was wounded in action on several occasions. Before he went to Viet Nam he asked his best friend to occasionally look in on his wife and young son to make sure they were all right. And his best friend agreed to do that. Three days after being discharged his wife informed him that she would be leaving him, divorcing him, and would be marrying his best friend. What a welcome home, what a reward for Dan for the fine job he had done.

***

Graig

Craig was trained in one the Army's Special Forces units, and just a few days before graduating he washed out. He spent most of the rest of his tour of duty in Germany. On being discharge he flew commercial jet back to the United States. At the first airport he arrived there were protestors that greeted him and one of them spit on him in the face. This was a common experience by many returning G.I.'s. About the worst case of mistreatment of returning G.I.'s was Steve. Steve returned to the U.S., via commercial aircraft, arrived at one of the United States better known airports. There he was greeted by protestors, one of who urinated on Steve's boots. Steve had to be restrained by two M.P.'s. What is most ironic is that these protestors were supposedly protesting the Viet Nam War and trying to bring the G.I.'s home, and how did they greet the G.I.'s who were returning, by spitting on them. What were they really protesting and whom were they really trying to help, it certainly was not the returning G.I.'s.

***

Jeff

Jeff was attached to a Deep Recon Unit. His mission in Viet Nam was to be dropped behind enemy lines to eliminate specific targets (people). Jeff was a sniper with dozens of confirmed kills and scores of unconfirmed kills. His assignments were selected for him; they were not his by choice. One time his assignment was to kill the mayor of a village and wait a few days, for the funeral. Then he was to kill a North Vietnamese dignitary, when he came to the funeral. The dignitary was a close friend of the mayor and the real target. He did his job very well and eventually the enemy placed a price on his head, "dead or alive." The reward would have been many, many thousands of dollars. At times, after accomplishing his mission, he would be required to lay perfectly still while the enemy was only a few feet away. He even recalls, on a few occasions, being stepped on by the enemy. Remember that this was the assignment the Marine Corps gave him and they trained him to do his job well. Jeff slept with a loaded 45 at his side and even in his hand on occasion, until the day he died.

**

Dave

Dave was in a tank unit in Viet Nam. His unit operated in areas where they used Agent Orange. Yes, he now suffers because of his contact with Agent Orange. For years he has been going to the local V.A. Hospital of gold treatments several times per week. The gold attracts impurities and is discharged through the urinary tract. He will continue to have to have these treatments for the rest of his life. How do we thank him for enduring the pain he has endured for the rest of his life? How do those that authorized the use of Agent Orange tell him they are sorry for what they allowed to happen to him? Note: Agent Orange, a defoliate agent that was used in the Viet Nam War. The troops were never told how deadly it really was, and they were allowed to play with it. Many would use squirt guns to play with it. Many have lost their lives due to the effects of Agent Orange, and many are still suffering from the painful effects of it. The treatment theyfound to help was gold injections, which attract impurities in the body thatAgent Orange introduced. The treatments are very painful, but without them those suffering will die sooner.

***

Bill

Bill was a Navy Seal, who was trained to operate deep behind enemy lines, where "silence was golden." He was trained in the use of the knife. The knife that saved his life on more than one occasion he nicknamed "Fred." Fred is closer to him than any friend could ever be. He had to be trained in the skillful use of the knife. Because of what he was asked to do, he now has to live with those memories for the rest of his life.

***

David

David, a Navy Corpsman, assigned to a Marine Group, cannot sleep well at night. To this day he continues to recall the time he spent in foxholes, deep in the jungle. Often he wakes up at night reliving the time when the enemy sneaked upon the fox hole next to his, killed the five Marines in that fox hole and cut the head off of one of them, while the others slept. Can you imagine waking up and seeing that and then living the rest of your life thinking, "That could have been me?" David often wondered why it wasn't his head that was cut off, as he said it could have been! David spent much of his tour of duty attached to Marine Squads, operating in the jungles of Viet Nam. He has continuing nightmares of a little girl's head rolling between his legs. Because of his many experiences he has continuing nightmares. He also sleeps with a loaded handgun at his side, wakes at the slightest noise. After returning from Viet Nam and being discharged he decided to go back to school, on the G.I. Bill. There were three lines to register for classes; one of them was the Veterans Line, which David was in with his wife. A young woman who couldn't have even been five foot tall nor weighed 100 pounds came up to David, while he was standing in a line, and pointed her forefinger in his chest and said, "You baby killer. How many babies did you kill in Viet Nam?" Fortunately, David's wife grabbed him by the arm to restrain him. Editor's note: Several vets whom I have talked with several who have waited in the veteran's lines, to register for classes at various colleges that have had similar experiences as David above. It is sad to say, but this was not an uncommon occurrence. David passed away on May 7, 1996, now he has that restful sleep he could never get after returning from war, and the firearm once at his side is finally gone. What is sad is that not one member from his family (immediate or extended) attended his memorial service.

***

Spike

Spike was a soldier who served one tour of duty in Viet Nam, many times in the jungles. He learned to survive, during his tour of duty, by being very alert to what was going on around him. His every instinct he used to survive. He had to learn to react to any given situation, in an instant. There was no time to think. You either acted on the spot or were killed. After his last patrol, he was sent back to the States to be discharged, honorably, his tour of duty was over! Within three days after leaving Viet Nam, he was discharged. When you are discharged you are in uniform. After receiving his discharge papers he went to the local airport, to rent a car, so he could get back home. When he arrived at the airport he was met by a group of hippies, who harassed him by calling him names and other things. He went to the car rental section, all the time this same group of hippies following him and harassing him. He continued to ask them to leave him alone! He got the keys to his rental car, and proceeded to go to the car, all the time this group of harassing hippies were following him. Finally he got to the car, still being harassed by that group of hippies, and he continued to ask them to leave him alone. The harassment became so heavy that he told them to leave or he would kill them. One of the members of that longhaired hippie group then proceeded to come up to Spike and seriously harasses him. Spike asked him to just leave him alone. But, that hippie wouldn't. Then the hippie spit in Spikes face. That act drove Spike over the edge and he hit that longhaired hippie so hard in the chest, with the car keys, that he drove a key into the hippie's heart, killing him. Spike was arrested and was sentenced to fifteen years in prison, for killing that hippie. What a way to welcome Spike back. That was his reward. He spent fifteen years in prison, for reacting to the situation as he had been trained act upon without thinking. Why did they not leave Spike alone? Why did they have to push him over the edge? Spike served his country well! What was his reward for putting his life on the line for a year in hell, and then fifteen years of hell in prison? The end result of spikes story was when, a couple of years after being released from prison, he stepped in front of and "kissed a train!" What caused Spike to commit suicide, was it the hell he went through in War, or was it the "Hell" he went through when he came back home? Many a Viet Nam Vet has died as a result of suicide, in fact more have died from suicide that died in the war! What drives them to do that? Is it the War they fought over there, or is it the War they fought back home, after returning? For those of you that choose to say it was not a war, ask all those who returned with Purple Hearts, or came back in "Body Bags" if it was a "War!"

***

John

Men healthy, with a bright future, were the ones the government took from society to fight in the Viet Nam War, which proved to be the most unpopular war the United States has ever fought. They took boys and men from society so that they could fight in a war, a war the government supported. They took those peace-loving, God-fearing men, and trained them and gave them the skills to fight, kill, and survive in a hostile land. Then they sent these men to fight in a war. Eventually the government did give those men back to society (they didn't give any boys back to society), but what did they give back? Did they give back young, Godfearing men, with a bright future ahead of them? Some they gave back in body bags, with no future at all. Others they gave back all beaten and battered and certainly they were not healthy, and their future looked bleak. Others they gave back and forever they would have to be treated for the wounds without scars. Others they gave back who would be considered derelicts and they would be destitute for the rest of their lives. Others they gave back, who would continue to do what they had been trained in war to do.

These would end up in prison for crimes against society, but those crimes considered crimes against society were not crimes in war at all. The government, mostly, gave back to society men with no future at all. For some their future was something they would have to fight for, for the rest of their lives. The government gave back to society very few that were Godfearing at all and too many of those would never be God fearing again. The government freely took from society, but they were unwilling to give back to society men like they had taken men who were young, healthy, God fearing and with the prospect of a bright future.

The following occurred on a public transportation bus ride, on a day I thought would be like all the others I had taken. It started out the same as all the other days, quiet and no one talking to one another. No one was speaking and all were deep within thoughts of their own. A few stops after I got on, a man stepped up on the bus. At first glance he appeared unshaven, wearing raggedy clothes, not had a bath in a few days, and was obviously hung over from the night before. He was my age.

When he first stepped on the bus he was loudly mumbling, but not dangerous to anyone at all. Yet, there was something about this man that drew my attention toward him. Some could have thought he was boisterous, and it appeared that he rambled from subject to subject, but he really didn't. It did not take long, and I heard him mention Richard Millhouse Nixon (President of the United States during the Viet Nam War). At that point I was sure he had been drafted and received a draft notice with President Nixon's signature on it. Then he started talking about the Mekong Delta. It was at that point that I knew for sure he was a Viet Nam vet.

As I listened to John, the name he mentioned was his, I started to think. Most of society looks down on John and certainly most on the bus would have rather had John somewhere else, than on that bus. Society in general has forgotten the war John fought in. But, John, will never be able to forget the war he fought in- even though it was over twenty-five years ago. Where John is today is a result of where he was in the Viet Nam War. Society, in general, cannot understand what John went through, nor do they want to understand. Most can't even imagine what John saw then and still sees today. Society today chooses to ignore the fact that John would not be what he is today if he had not been asked to fight in that War. Society, in general, would like to ignore the bad side effects that war brings for those who fight and there are bad side effects of which John is one.

Before John was drafted, he had the potential to be a productive member of society (or at least what society considers productive) and probably to become a man that would have been respected by society. But, because John is what he is he is not liked by society, in fact he is scorned by society, and society doesn't like him. John's case even hit a little closer to him, for me. I wondered how far I am from being like John. It certainly would have been easy for me to be like John, and I would have been just as detested as John is today. John got off the bus at the stop nearest the first tavern that opened on the route, and it was obvious what was going to happen- a repeat of the previous d ay. As I got out off the bus, I couldn't help but think that I now had to give the appearance of being NORMAL, so that I would be accepted by society. As I thought even more, I wondered how normal are John and I? How much different are John and I? Society accepts one of us, but not the other—or do they really not accept either one of us?

Many looked at John and wondered, "How could he become like that?"

I looked at John and wondered, "Why didn't I become like John?"

The government took John in his prime, when he was at his best and this is what the government gave back. Does the government not have any shame? John was used and when his usefulness was over, he was thrown back to society, to the wolves. No matter what John became, or whatever any returning vet becomes, society will always owe them a debt of gratitude that cannot be paid back. Even to this day John and all vets should be respected for answering the call when their country called!

***

Adam

There are many stories that can be told about those who fought in the Viet Nam War, both on the side of the United States and Viet Nam. This story is about a Lieutenant in the Army of the Republic of Viet Nam (South Viet Nam). I met Lim in an Albertson's Store in Seattle, WA. He was stocking the donut shelf. I was there to pick up an order of donuts. He noticed the ballcap I was wearing with my Dolphin Pin. He asked me if I was a vet.

I replied, "Yes, the Viet Nam War."

He said, "Me too. I was a Lieutenant in the Army of the Republic of Viet Nam."

I told him I was happy to see he made it out alive. We shook hands and hugged. Then he asked me how my health was and I told him that it was as good as could be expected. Then he told me that in 1975 (after Saigon fell) he was placed in a Communist Concentration Camp for seven years. He said he had been greatly mistreated in that camp and now suffers serious health problems because of his internment in that camp. We returning vets (to the

United States) feel we were greatly mistreated after returning from the war. Those who served in the South Vietnamese Army suffered even more at the hands of the communists, after the fall of Saigon.

Adam, who owns and operates a small shop in Seattle where I frequent, is from Viet Nam and is about sixty years old (1999). After I got to know him I asked him where he was from and he told me Viet Nam. He shared his story with me about being a Lieutenant in the South Vietnamese Army and after the United States pulled out of Viet Nam he was captured and spent many years in a "re-education" camp. He didn't want to talk much about life in re-education camps. I eventually asked him how he managed to come to the United States. He told me that in 1985 he escaped from Viet Nam on a small boat. His small boat was eventually sighted by a U.S. Naval Vessel and all occupants were taken onboard the U.S. Vessel. He was eventually sent to the Philippines, where he spent two years in a refugee camp. Then he immigrated to the United States and he settled in the Seattle area. I asked him if he had been back to Viet Nam and he told me he had been there several times. He related that all of his relatives (children included) still live in Viet Nam. I asked him if he was ever going to return to Viet Nam to live with his family.

He said "No."

Naturally, I asked him, "Why?"

His reply was very simple and required no explanation. "FREEDOM. We have freedom here, and now that I have tasted freedom I don't want to give it up."

What a powerful statement. Freedom. I wonder how many born in the United States value their freedom as much as Adam values the freedom he now has?

***

William (Buddy) Leander Erikson, Jr.

No section, such as this would be complete without talking about those that were killed in the Viet Nam War. There were over 58,000 plus that died in Viet Nam. Now, their names are forever on a wall in Washington, D.C. But, all we see are their names; most do not know what any of these individuals were like. I knew one very well and his name was William Leander Erikson, Jr., whom we all called "Buddy" during our high school days. I knew him well because he only lived a few housesfrom. We lived about one mile from the high school and walked home from school together. I will now tell "Buddy's" story because he was typical ofthe many that lost their lives in that war. Buddy was an only child. Buddy was the kind of person that was friends with everybody. He didn't have any enemies because he never did anything to upset other people. He was a kind person to all. He was not an athlete and he did not turn out for any sports during high school. He was not a scholar and he didn't receive any scholarship to go to college. As most would look at Buddy he was not the kind of person that anything stood out. He didn't have any special talents, or so people generally thought, and he did very little in extracurricular activities after school. He was just "good people."

As we walked home together we would talk about all kinds of things. I can never remember him ever speaking ill about anyone else. We would joke around and tell jokes. Buddy was very good at making up jokes. We were typical kids we would run, chase one another, and also play tag, while we were walking home. We also, occasionally, would talk about serious topics, for instance, what we wanted to do in the future, after we graduated from high school. Buddy looked forward to getting a job, eventually getting married, having children and raising a family. We never once talked about Viet Nam or the draft; those things were so far away and distant that we didn't concern ourselves with them. Buddy looked forward to the normal things in life, as did I. We graduated from high school in June of 1966. Shortly after we graduated Buddy received his draft notice and was drafted into the Army. Shortly after arriving in Viet Nam he was killed. One of the saddest things about Buddy being killed was that it was not in Buddy's nature to kill anyone, he was harmless. And yet, this harmless man lost his life. Buddy was never old enough to vote, but he was not too young to die. Buddy never did get a chance to marry, have children, and raise a family. As I stated earlier, Buddy was an only child and his parents never did get to have any grandchildren. Most of those who died in Viet Nam were like Buddy. I did not know all the 58,000, but I did know Buddy and I will never forget him and now no one else will forget him. Buddy, and all those that died, is not a faceless name on a wall. He was a real person who lived and loved life. He had goals, but he never lived long enough to even try to accomplish even one of the goals he had setout to do. I miss you Buddy and I am so sorry that you lost your life!

Here is something for all to think about. Buddy's life ended before he was twenty. So Buddy's lifetime was twenty years. I now have lived almost three of Buddy's lifetimes. I have had the chance to do all the things that Buddy never had a chance to do. I often think of what Buddy would have become if he had not been killed. I often wonder why Buddy was killed and I survived. Buddy was not mean, and I can't say that about me. I many times ponder what if Buddy had lived and I had been killed, what difference in the world would Buddy have made, that I never did make?

Buddy was only one of over 58,000 that lost their lives in the Viet Nam War. I often think of the 58,000 and what they would have become if they had not been killed in that war? Who among them would have become President of the United States? Who among them would have gone on to become Olympic stars? Who among them would have gone on to win the Pulitzer Prize? Who among them would have went on to become great scientist and made life saving discoveries? Who among them would have went on to become great doctors and saved the lives of many? Who among them would have gone on to become great athletics, even superstars? Who among them would have gone onto become outstanding business leaders? And then I ponder how much did we really loose by the death of those that were killed? What great losses we really had, because we will never know what their true potential was! Now, I have to become the best I can become so that their lives were not wasted! Because I have the chance to become the best I can become, I must become the best I can because they never had the chance to become the best they could become!

***

Bob

I was faced with being drafted in to the Army or Marines, leaving for Canada or enlisting in the Navy. In 65. I chose the Navy. I was made a Radarman on a DD... the first ship hit by North Vietnamese shore fire. Two dead, four wounded one very seriously. We had an excellent full Captain. We did suppression of logistics from the North by the sea and close support of our troops from the fish hooks north to the DMZ. I was a Combat Information Center Wartime Supervisor of CIC and one of the Gunfire Support Navigators, meaning I put the 5 inch guns on target. The ship was credited with close to 3000 enemy KIA. In a typhoon my spine was fractured, the VA doesn't want to pay a cent and has faked my records and worse. I don't trust them as far as I can spit. Bless our crew and someday what we did might be able to be told.

***

Dennis

I dealt with some crappy attitudes from those who served before in other wars... and of course those who protested and hated the war. The deal is many had no choice but to serve. I have had much time to think about Viet Nam after getting out and the past two much time. I am sorry so many lives were lost serving in that war that perhaps they wanted no part of. I love our country... but not always in agreement with what the old men in power come up with. My job in the Navy was great.

Thinking of the Veterans who have served and currently serve. God Bless. Thank You for Your Service! I served as a Dental Tech aboard a CVA-1967, off the coast of Viet Nam. At when times when I would go up to the fantail to dump the garbage—I could see from the ship the reality that a war was going on—smoke, flames from bombs. My thoughts are with those who currently serve and have served—some paying the ultimate price for serving our country.

***

Bau

One day I was talking to Bau and he brought up something that I had not thought about. It was a side of the Viet Nam War that has been neglected and it is a story that needs to be told.

There is nothing that can compare to what the life of the South Vietnamese soldiers went through after the United States withdrew (1975). Many died because of revenge, and many more died in re-education camps.

You guys have done more damage than you can ever imagine. Let me explain. We spent 1000-years fighting back to regain our independence from China. Let me repeat 1,000-years of slavery from the Chinese. Then the Mongols came for another 300 years, slavery again after Chinese left. Then we got a few breaks for a little while. Then the French came and continued slavery for another 100 years. Then Japanese, and then British, and then we thought America was the savior we had hoped for. It turned out the United States sold us back to China again. Now we are Chinese slaves. They come into Viet Nam to do whatever they want to the Vietnamese people because they have the communist Viet Nam leader protect them and to pay for the debt incurred to the Chinese government during the Viet Nam War. Just picture if the North had sold the Southern States back to British after the Revolutionary War? The Chinese are living in Viet Nam right now. They have taken the land and do whatever they want. Also about 50,000 children of mixed race (U.S. Soldiers and Vietnamese women), left behind and abandon at a young age to fend for themselves.

Appendix II: Charlie and the Last Job

I will conclude the story section with the last job I had. I mostly worked for others throughout my working career. It started in about 1962 hauling hay for local farmers in Prineville, Oregon. I will describe "hauling hay," for those that don't know what I am talking about. The work started after they hay had been raked and then bailed into about one-hundred-pound bales, give or take twenty pounds depending on how much tensions had been set on the baler. Usually, it was always over one hundred pounds and not less than a hundred. When we would get to a field, where the baled hay was, it was our job to "buck" the bails from the ground onto the bed of a flatbed, two-ton truck. Then someone upon the bed would carefully stack the bails on top of one another, stacking them so they crisscrossed so they didn't come falling down. When the bails were stacked six or seven rows high then it was time to drive the truck to the hay shed or barn. We would buck the bails off the truck onto the ground. Then jump off the bed of the truck onto the ground and start stacking the bails on top of one another until they were about fifteen to twenty rows high in the shed. It actually depended on the height of the shed how high the bails were stacked. It was all done by hand and those that couldn't hack the work were called "marshmallows." I did that three or four summers while I was in high school.

Next, I worked on a surveying crew for the summer, to put me through three quarters at the University. Next, I had various summer jobs and part time jobs to defray my expenses to go to college. I always made enough and scrutinized what I made to make it last three more quarters at the University. Then it was off to the Navy for six years. Then back to civilian life and working to provide for myself and my family.

I worked for a lot of companies (over forty to be exact) during my fifty years after the Navy. My employment was split between contract and direct jobs, and for about fifteen years of that time I had multiple jobs at the same time. I started working for the last company in July of 2012, when I was sixty-five, when most people are retiring. As the years went by, at the last company, people would retire, and the company would always give them a 'retirement' party. After five years I began to look forward to my retirement party. I never complained about anything while I was there. There were times when I would put in a 24-hour day, because a job had to go the next day. I would always arrive at the office at 4:30 am, even though my work time didn't start until 6:30 am. I never put those hours, from 4:30-6:30 am, on my timecard—it was my contribution to help the company grow. That routine went on for eight years.

I never once complained about only getting one pay raise during that ten-year period, because I didn't think I should have to ask for a pay raise. It was something I thought companies should give to deserving people. If they didn't think I deserved a pay raise it was okay, because I at least still had a job. In 2020 Covid-19 hit and that changed the workplace. I, along with others, was asked to work remotely. I voice my opinion that I would rather stay in the office. That fell on deaf ears. From the end of March 2021 to April 2023 I worked remotely and found that I liked it and it really didn't matter if I was banging away on a computer in the office, or on my computer at home, I could do the job just as well either place. The difference was it didn't cost me any "gas" money to walk from upstairs to downstairs where my computer was. I was tied into the office network and stayed in daily communication with the office via email and Teams. I never cheated that company, or any company, out of wages. I only put hours I actually worked on my timecard, not time I was waiting around to get work. Toward the end I was really starting to look forward to retiring and having a retirement party. It would be a last hurrah at the company.

The first week in April 2023 I received an email message that my immediate supervisor and a Human Resources person wanted to meet with me on a Teams Call. I thought, well I guess I am going to be asked to return to the office, like many others had been asked to do. I guess I have to accept the inevitable, was my thought. Surely if they were going to let me go, they would have me come into the office so they could do that 'face-to-face.'

I guess I did have some apprehensions about the real reason for the Teams Meeting, because normally when your supervisor and HR meet with you it is either a promotion or you are being let go. Meeting time came and I was right online when I was supposed to be. Both my supervisor and HR were ready. After the usual pleasantries were said it was right down to the business at hand. My supervisor quickly got to the task at hand. He said there wasn't enough work to keep me on the payroll. HR piped up and said all that I was owed would be put in my bank account the following Friday. They caught me off guard. I was being fired from the last job I would ever have. They hit me pretty hard, but I didn't let them know that what they did really hurt, way deep down. That meant that I wasn't even worthy of a retirement party, after being with the company over ten years. They could have just as easily given me the choice of retiring from the company. But, no I was fired; call it what you want but I call it being fired. In less than fifteen minutes it was over, but the hurt of being let go the way I was will last for a long time.

Here is the clincher. I was completely disconnected from the company servers fifteen minutes after we hung up, and my access to company email was severed. I wasn't even given a chance to say goodbye to the friends I had made during the over ten years I worked for the company. I was completely shut out. Talk about feeling like a criminal. I suppose a companywide message was sent out saying that I had decided to leave the company and/or maybe they even wrote I had decided to retire. I hope they will never again treat anyone like I was treated on my last day. If you are going to let someone go, for whatever reason, do it face-to-face, not on a Teams or Zoom call, or even on the phone. If a person is over sixty-five and you want to let them go give them the option of retiring first, before you let them go. I would have jumped at that opportunity to officially retire. Now, whenever I am asked if I am retired, I cannot say yes, because I was fired from my last job. I didn't retire from the company. I just say "I am no longer working for anybody else. My time is my own." When you let anyone go let them retain some dignity in being let go. Let them say their goodbyes. Let them clean out their personal belongings. Let them walk out with their heads held high! Don't make them regret ever working for you!

Appendix III: Useful Websites

United Vibes, posting pictures of those Killed in Action and the date they were killed. What were you doing on the day they were killed? What have you been able to do since they were killed that they never had a chance to do?

https://www.facebook.com/vibes.united

Appendix IV: Helpful Numbers

Disabled Veterans

https://benefits.va.gov/BENEFITS/benefits-summary/SummaryofVABene-fitsforDisabledVeterans.pdf

https://988lifeline.org/

If you need to talk, the 988 Lifeline is there. "At the 988 Suicide & Crisis Life-line, we understand that life's challenges can sometimes be difficult. Whether you're facing mental health struggles, emotional distress, alcohol or drug use concerns, or just need someone to talk to, our caring counselors are here for you. You are not alone."

Call - Text - Chat - Deaf/HoH

Appendix V: Recommended Reading List

This is my recommended reading list for excellent authors who wrote outstanding books on the Viet Nam Conflict, or as the Vietnamese called it, the "American War."

Bare Feet, Iron Will: Stories from the Other Side of Vietnam's Battlefields by James G. Zumwalt

This was the review I wrote on Mr. Zumwalt's book.

Bare Feet, Iron Will by James G. Zumwalt is a very touching book and it reached right down through my brain, past my emotions and then deep into my heart. His book is one of my rare 1-day books; in less than 24-hour straight I started and finished reading the book. The book is superbly written. I am a Vietnam War Draftee, who chose to enlist in the Navy (20 Jun 1969) rather than be drafted into the Armed Forces (24 Jun 1969). Mr. Zumwalt (out of respect for him and not obligation) opened of the floodgates of my emotions. His book about the "other side" of the war proved not to be the other side, but in fact all sides. But, there was a big difference between both sides. Americans had to turn on their TV's and watch the newscast and read the newspapers to learn what was going on in Viet Nam. However, as Mr. Zumwalt so eloquently points out, the Vietnamese didn't have to turn on their TV's; all they had to do was look outside their front windows, hear the bombs dropping and then exploding and many time knowing family and friends were vaporized. All the Vietnamese wanted was to be free and independent, which Mr. Zumwalt proves to the utmost any author can. Yes, I did shed tears as I read at the loss of 58,000+ American Troops. But, I shed even more tears at the loss of over 1-million North Vietnamese and Viet Cong soldiers, and the loss of more than 254,000 South Vietnamese servicemen, and the loss more than 2-million Vietnamese Civilians, and the Vietnamese that are still suffering from the effects of Agent Orange, and all those needlessly suffering from Napalm burnings. Then to realize Mr. Zumwalt was right in pointing out that Ho Chi Minh was our Ally during WWII in fighting the Japanese. All Ho Chi Minh wanted was freedom and independence and if he would have been given it in 1945 think of all the death, destruction, and needless losses that would have been avoid because he posthumously got what he wanted 30 years later. Thank you Mr. Zumwalt for your eye opening and accurate appraisal of the War in Viet Nam. I salute you Sir and compliment you. Job Well Done.

Snow in Vietnam: A Novel by Amy M. Le

Snow in Seattle: A Novel by Amy M. Le

Snow's Kitchen: A Novella and Cookbook by Amy M. Le

Amy M. Le's books, known as the "*Snow Trilogy,*" are marvelously written and only someone that lived through it could have written the "story" so well. They may be novels, however I would call them Historical Fiction, because only the names were changed (to protect the innocent?). Each of those books were a 1-day book read for me, read in less than a 24-hour sitting.

I highly recommend these three books for those that want to learn more about the plight of refugees coming to this country and the plight of veterans returning home from a very unpopular war. Amy has broached a subject that has been kept quiet for far too long.

Hidden Agendas by John Pilger

Heroes by John Pilger

Soldier by Anthony B. Herbert, Lt. Col., Ret.
  Why Viet Nam? Prelude to America's Albatross by Archimedes L.A. Patti

  JFK: The CIA, Viet Nam, and the Plot to Assassinate John F. Kennedy by L. Fletcher Prouty (2011), Chapter Four "Viet Nam: The Opening Wedge" (pages 42-50).

"I can handle being abused and mistreated.

I can handle those who swear at me and belittled me.

I can handle those who are nasty and mean.

What I cannot handle are those who are kind to me,

It brings me to my knees every time." —Anonymous

About the Author

Charlie Peters has been married for 50 years and has four children, nine grandchildren, and thirteen great-grandchildren. He accidentally started writing poetry in 1990 and discovered that poetry proved to be an outlet to release the frustration of PTSD symptoms. He wrote poetry for about ten years. Two of his poems were runner-ups in national poetry contests: "A Man Less Than His Best" and "Stairway." Then he shifted his writing efforts to political commentary and satire, and two of his published books resulted from those commentaries: "The National Debt? The Sinking of America!" (2008) and "TEA Time Has Arrived 'We the People' Versus Washington Bureaucracy." (2009). He has now decided to publish many of the poems he wrote in the 1990s, and this book is a result of his poetry writing.

"Returning Vet's Saga: The Healing Power of Poetry" is a work that may appeal to those suffering from unexplained moments of anger, frustration, frightening nightmares, and unexplained moments of depression, which a downpouring of tears may accompany. The author experienced all of those symptoms after returning from the military, and the symptoms lasted for about fifteen years before those symptoms even had a name, which we now call "PTSD." The author found that a sound, a smell, a spoken word, another person's voice inflection, or something as simple as a commercial on television can trigger an episode of PTSD.

There is no magic in poetry. However, the magic comes in putting feelings to paper, coming directly from the heart and completely bypassing the brain. We may not think of ourselves as poets, but if we just let the words flow, we may find that we are, in fact, poets of a special kind.

This book ends with the poem that got it all started.

Charlie Peters

www.ingramcontent.com/pod-product-compliance
Lightning Source LLC
Chambersburg PA
CBHW071719120626
46550CB00001B/296